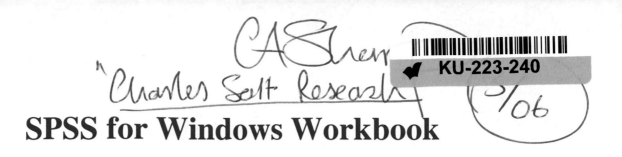

SPSS for Windows Workbook

to accompany

Tabachnick and Fidell

Using Multivariate Statistics

Fourth Edition

Prepared by

Steven J. Osterlind
University of Missouri-Columbia

Barbara G. Tabachnick
California State University, Northridge

Allyn and Bacon
Boston   London   Toronto   Sydney   Tokyo   Singapore

Table of Contents

List of Figures

List of Output

Preface

Thanks are due to the numerous reviewers—particularly students who were patient through incomplete drafts of the workbook and suffered through errors, who pointed out problems with the draft versions, and who provided a multitude of helpful suggestions leading to improvement. Especially, thanks are due to Chris Mahmood, Rhonda Wood, John Hagar, Renita Coleman, Chris Beaudoin and others who worked through the examples, with text and data sets in hand, and helped us avoid numerous embarrassments. Remaining errors, of course, are ours.

We also thank Linda Fidell, co-author of the text, for her friendship, inspiration, and general good cheer. She is all that one could want in a collaborator, colleague and friend. And, finally, we'd like to thank our respective spouses—husband Ken, and wife Nancy—for their patience and continuing support.

Steven J. Osterlind
Barbara G. Tabachnick

Chapter 1. Introduction

This workbook demonstrates analyses of the complete examples of each chapter in *Using Multivariate Statistics*, 4th edition (Tabachnick and Fidell, 2001) through SPSS for Windows, version 10.0. As a workbook, it augments *UMS* and is not a "stand alone" publication. When working through these demonstrations of the *UMS* complete examples, it may be necessary to have both publications open to the apposite pages.

The chapters of this workbook follow those in the main text with some early exceptions in Chapters 1, 2, and 3. The first three chapters of *UMS* review basic statistical concepts for univariate and multivariate procedures and do not use the complete examples. In this workbook, Chapter 2 provides a quick guide to the techniques presented in subsequent chapters, and Chapter 3 offers an overview of SPSS for Windows, reviewing basic procedures for opening SPSS system files in SPSS for Windows. Chapters 4 through 16 are parallel to the complete examples in *UMS*.

Working through *UMS* with this workbook requires specific data files. *UMS*, 4th edition, does not have an accompanying disk with the data files; instead the appropriate files can be accessed via the Internet at http://www.abacon.com/tabachnick. The files are in two formats. First, they are provided in SPSS format, with a "*.sav" suffix (or "extension") where the * indicates a wildcard that can be any legitimate file name. It is recommended that you use these files since they are directly accessible to the SPSS program. Additionally, files are also provided as comma-delimited, text files (i.e., ASCII), with a *.csv suffix for persons who may need access to the raw data but who do not have the SPSS program. Section 3.1 of Chapter 3 provides detailed instruction on how to access and open the files in both formats.

Each chapter of this workbook begins by identifying the applicable data file. Thereafter, the information follows the presentation of the complete example in the corresponding chapter of the main text, *Using Multivariate Statistics*, 4th edition. Appendix B of *UMS* provides pertinent information about the variables in the data sets and the study from which the data derives. Students are strongly encouraged to familiarize themselves with the study.

As noted, this workbook conforms to version 10.0 of SPSS and requires the SPSS statistical routines of the Base, Advanced, and Professional modules. Persons using versions 8.x or 9.x will be able to follow most presentations in this workbook with appropriate adaptations for the prior versions of the program.

SPSS, Inc., with version 10.0, effectively created two editions of the SPSS program, one for "clients" and another for "servers." In common usage, a client is a single user machine that is not running SPSS from a network. If you purchased SPSS and installed it on your own personal computer, and you are not accessing the program through a network, then you are regarded as a "client." The server edition of SPSS is useful to network administrators who may have many users across the network accessing the same program. Functionally, version 10.0 of SPSS is the same as versions 9.x. Persons running version 8.0 can still use this workbook with accommodation for the later versions. Versions of SPSS earlier than 8.0 are not suitable for guidance by this workbook.

Also, SPSS, Inc., has reinstituted its support for the Macintosh platform with a version 10.x compatible with the Macintosh operating system. Persons using the supported Macintosh versions can also use this workbook, as the routines, menus, and dialog boxes for Macintosh are nearly identical to those in Windows. Of course, Macintosh users running SPSS for Windows under emulation will have the usual DOS-based Windows interface.

It is presumed that users of this workbook have installed SPSS on a computer and are familiar with the Windows environment, including knowing how to use the various Help facilities (e.g., Help menu, What's This?, and Results Coach). Students will find the *SPSS Syntax Guide* (included with the Student Edition as an electronic file) also helpful but not necessary for this workbook. Persons new to SPSS are encouraged to review the SPSS Tutorial (available through the main Help menu) as an introduction to the program.

So, in conclusion, have the program installed, access the files on the Web, and have the main text for *UMS* open in front of you along with this workbook, and let's begin!

Chapter 2. A Guide to Statistical Techniques

The contents of Chapters 1 through 3 of this workbook are described in the previous chapter. Chapter 4 illustrates SPSS setups and some of the output for screening ungrouped and grouped data sets from the complete example in Chapter 4 of *UMS*. Data screening techniques are referenced throughout this workbook as well as in many places in *UMS*. Additionally, because data screening is useful to all of the procedures in *UMS*, its techniques are presented in greater detail than are some other statistics. Hence, it is a good idea to carefully work through this chapter before proceeding to the others. Thereafter, the chapters need not necessarily be studied in order; but rather, users can turn to any particular chapter of interest for information on a statistical technique. One caution, however, when using the chapters out of order: often information necessary for a given technique relies upon knowledge presented in the preceding chapters.

Chapter 5 describes SPSS setups and some output for standard and hierarchical multiple regression. Chapter 6 demonstrates canonical correlation. Chapter 7 shows how to do hierarchical log linear analysis. Chapter 8 presents analysis of covariance. Chapter 9 demonstrates setups and outputs for multivariate analysis of variance and covariance examples. Chapter 10 makes clear how to do profile analysis of repeated measures. Chapter 11 illustrates an example of direct discriminant function analysis. Chapter 12 demonstrates direct logistic regression analysis with two outcomes. Chapter 13 shows how to do a principal factor analysis. Chapter 14 introduces structural equation modeling (SEM). SPSS has no direct capability for SEM, but several SEM programs are available. One such SEM program, called AMOS (for **A**nalysis of **MO**ment **S**tructures, and produced by SmallWaters, Inc.), is distributed by SPSS. AMOS is available as an SPSS plug-in module or as a stand-alone program. This workbook uses AMOS v.4.0 for demonstration of SEM as well as for confirmatory factor analysis in Chapter14. Chapter 15 shows an example of a Cox regression survival analysis, and Chapter 16 shows a time series analysis with an intervention.

The computer procedures in this workbook correspond directly to those of the non-Windows setup and output in the text of *UMS* wherever possible; however, some of the complete examples in the main text are illustrated with statistical routines in programs other than SPSS. In those instances, the closest corresponding analysis through SPSS for Windows is shown.

Chapter 3. Overview of SPSS for Windows

SPSS allows one to easily perform basic univariate and multivariate analyses (including evaluation of many assumptions) for analysis of variance, for correlation, for regression, and more; and, it produces many varieties of plots and other graphics to display and help understand data. Many basic procedures are reviewed in Chapter 4 in the context of screening grouped and ungrouped data sets, and in other chapters in the context of requirements for specific multivariate analyses.

Some statistical procedures are unavailable directly through SPSS menus and dialog boxes. For example, in regression, some of the statistics that are available in batch mode do not appear among the menu options or toolbar buttons. In these instances, procedures for working with a simple syntax file are demonstrated. Techniques for working with syntax commands are illustrated in Chapters 5 and 7, as well as elsewhere throughout the workbook.

We begin our exploration into using SPSS for multivariate analysis by first seeing how SPSS works, and then we move to a description of the notations used in this workbook that succinctly show what SPSS menu choice and dialog box options should be selected.

A simple demonstration of how SPSS accesses summary descriptive statistics will illustrate how SPSS works. Begin by positioning the cursor over the **Analyze** command on the main menu in the **SPSS Data Editor** window (Figure 3.1). By holding down the left mouse button, a hierarchical submenu automatically pops up allowing several choices among statistical procedures. Moving the cursor over the choice **Descriptive Statistics** pops up another level submenu of choices for summarizing statistics (i.e., **Frequencies ... Descriptives...** etc.). Here, however, the options are followed by ellipses (. . .) indicating that a dialog box will follow. Dialog boxes present several choices within one domain and frequently selections include or preclude other choices. Precluded choices are automatically dimmed out to not permit them. Moving the cursor over the **Descriptives...** choice pops up the next dialog box, presenting an appropriate set of options (Figures 3.1, 3.2, and 3.3). This is the general structure of SPSS hierarical menu choice and dialog box options. Menus generally have submenus that lead to dialog boxes with many choices, each level becoming more specific to a particular statistical procedure or output.

We move now to a description of the notation used with this workbook to denote menu selections and choices in dialog boxes. Understanding how the notation works is essential to making sense of SPSS. In parallel fashion to hierarchical conventions within SPSS, the notation in this workbook also uses a hierarchical scheme, denoted by tabs and indented words. This means that each choice within SPSS is indented one tab further to indicate one deeper layer of choice. Main choices are preceded by a "greater than" symbol (>). SPSS option buttons (called "radio buttons") and check boxes are preceded by their own icons (i.e., ⊙ or ☑). Variable names are preceded by a bullet (•). Rectangular-shaped "push buttons" bring forth another dialog box and are identified by their own name. SPSS defaults are generally not cited and usually should remain as is.

An example of the notation of this workbook for SPSS choices is given on the following page, to the right side of Figures 3.1, 3.2, and 3.3. The figures themselves show the corresponding screen snapshots of the SPSS main menu, submenus, and dialog boxes. Take a moment to study this notation as it will be used throughout this workbook.

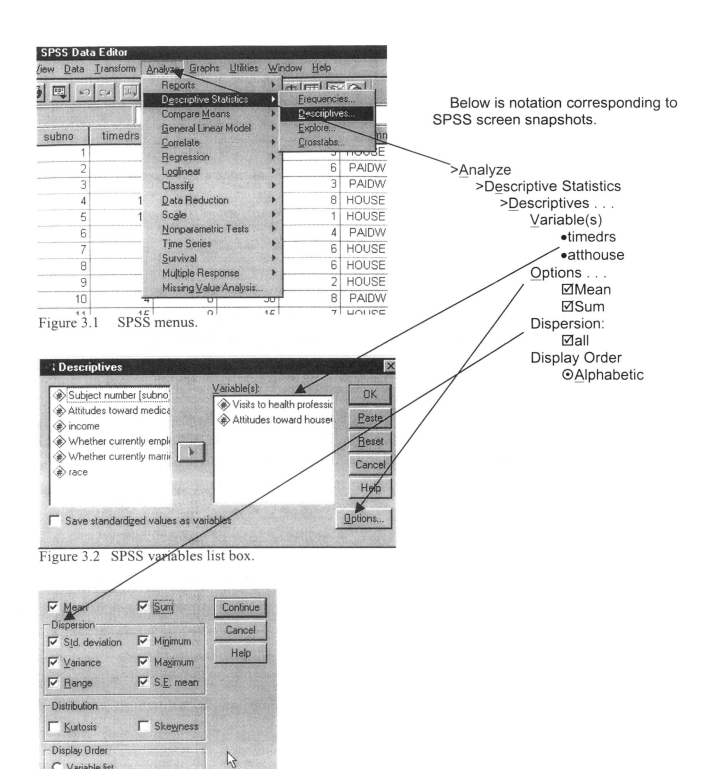

Figure 3.1   SPSS menus.

Figure 3.2   SPSS variables list box.

Figure 3.3   SPSS dialog box.

Below is notation corresponding to SPSS screen snapshots.

>Analyze
　>Descriptive Statistics
　　>Descriptives . . .
　　　Variable(s)
　　　　•timedrs
　　　　•atthouse
　　Options . . .
　　　☑Mean
　　　☑Sum
　　Dispersion:
　　　☑all
　　Display Order
　　　⊙Alphabetic

7

```
SUBNO,TIMEDRS,ATTDRUG,ATTHOUSE,INCOME,EMPLMNT,MSTATUS,RACE
1,1,8,27,5,1,2,1
2,3,7,20,6,0,2,1
3,0,8,23,3,0,2,1
4,13,9,28,8,1,2,1
5,15,7,24,1,1,2,1
6,3,8,25,4,0,2,1
7,2,7,30,6,1,2,1
8,0,7,24,6,1,2,1
9,7,7,20,2,1,2,1
10,4,8,30,8,0,1,1
11,15,9,15,7,1,2,1
```

Figure 3.5   Text (ASCII) file for data set: SCREEN.csv.

Users of previous versions of SPSS will welcome SPSS system changes in version 10 that allow a variety of formats (e.g., text, RTF, from Excel, SAS, BMD, SYSTAT, and others) to be read directly into the SPSS data editor. [Note: for some formats, SPSS opens an Import Wizard that guides you through a number of steps to import the data into appropriate columns.]

3.2 USING AND DEFINING DATA

Figure 3.6 displays the file "Screen" opened into the **SPSS Data Editor** window. The variables are listed in columns, each with its own name shown. (SPSS limits variable names to eight characters, either alpha or numeric). Cases (also called "records") are in the rows, shown in bold, black numbers along the left. For this data set, the first variable is named SUBNO to indicate a number for a given individual within the data set. Most data sets have a subject identifier; here as a sequence number, but often it is a social security number or other unique identifier. The SPSS case number may or may not be the same as the variable SUBNO. (Suppose, for example subject number 35 drops out of the study and her data are not used.)

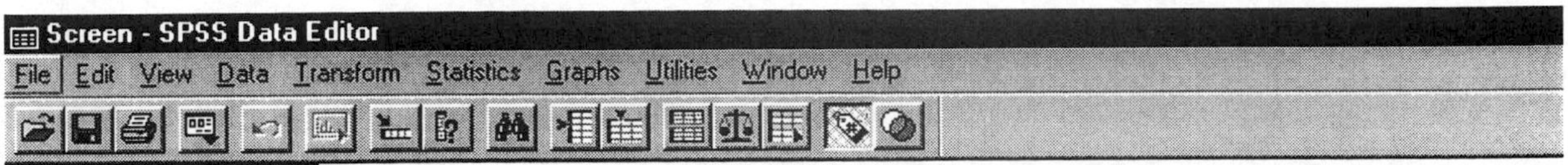

Screen - SPSS Data Editor

File Edit View Data Transform Statistics Graphs Utilities Window Help

	subno	timedrs	attdrug	atthouse	income	emplmnt	mstatus	race
1	1	1	8	27	5	HOUSEWF	2	1
2	2	3	7	20	6	PAIDWORK	2	1
3	3	0	8	23	3	PAIDWORK	2	1
4	4	13	9	28	8	HOUSEWF	2	1
5	5	15	7	24	1	HOUSEWF	2	1
6	6	3	8	25	4	PAIDWORK	2	1
7	7	2	7	30	6	HOUSEWF	2	1
8	8	0	7	24	6	HOUSEWF	2	1
9	9	7	7	20	2	HOUSEWF	2	1
10	10	4	8	30	8	PAIDWORK	1	1
11	11	15	9	15	7	HOUSEWF	2	1
12	12	0	6	22	3	HOUSEWF	2	1

Figure 3.6   "Screen" data in SPSS **Data Editor** window.

Also looking at the **SPSS Data Editor** window shown in Figure 3.6, you will notice that no values are displayed for the variable EMPLMNT; instead, descriptive words (called "value labels") are shown, making it easier to see the categories (e.g., HOUSEWF, PAIDWORK) for this variable. Of course, SPSS still employs a label's values (e.g., "0," "1") for calculations. For any variable, you can conveniently view either the values or a value's label, whichever you prefer. You must define for SPSS which view you prefer; and, of course, if you opt for the value labels view, you must also define for SPSS what labels to use with which value. Choosing a particular view of a variable requires only a simple point and click on the toolbar to activate or deactivate the "labels" icon. The labels toolbar icon is the second to the last icon on the right, looking something like a paper luggage tag. In Figure 3.6, the values label is turned on (i.e., highlighted). Alternatively, you may check or uncheck a view by selecting **View** from the main menu and then the **Value Labels** option. How to set labels for values in a variable is described momentarily, after some necessary background.

You may also have realized by now that there are two views in which to see Screen data (or any other data set) in the **SPSS Data Editor** window: a **Data View** and a **Variable View**. You select a view by clicking on one or the other of the tabs at the bottom of the **SPSS Data Editor** window. The available tabs are shown in Figure 3.7. Alternatively, from the **Data View** you may jump to the **Variable View** by clicking on a variable name (i.e., top of column); and, correspondingly, jump from **Variable View** to **Data View** by double-clicking on a variable's number, next to it's name.

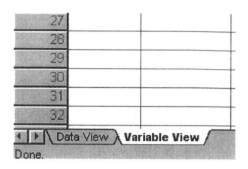

Figure 3.7   **Variable View** tab in
               Data Editor window.

Figure 3.8 shows the **Variable View** for Screen data.

Name	Type	Width	Decimals	Label	Values	Missing
subno	Numeric	3	0		None	None
timedrs	Numeric	3	0	Visits to health	None	None
attdrug	Numeric	3	0	Attitudes towar	None	None
atthouse	Numeric	3	0	Attitudes towar	None	1
income	Numeric	3	0	Income code	None	None
emplmnt	Numeric	3	0		{0, PAIDWOR	None
mstatus	Numeric	3	0	Current marital	None	None
race	Numeric	3	0	Ethnic affiliatio	None	None

Figure 3.8   **Variable View** of the **SPSS Data Editor** for Screen data.

You see in Figure 3.8 how SPSS organizes data. Data is defined by a number of "characteristics" which are displayed and can be modified in the **Variable View**. There are many characteristics for variables, such as the name you assign to it, whether the variable is alphabetic or numeric, the column width (useful when exporting data to other formats or programs), the number of decimals displayed, and more.

Returning to the value labels discussion, one sees that value labels are defined for variables in **Variable View**. To add a value label for a variable's numeric value (e.g., for EMPLMNT, "0" is displayed as "PAIDWORK" and "1" is displayed as "HOUSEWF"—cf. Figure 3.6), first, click on the cell showing the intersection of the **Values** column and the "EMPLMNT" row. This action makes shaded ellipses appear in the cell. Then, click the shaded ellipses and the **Value Labels** dialog box pops up. The **Value Labels** dialog box is shown in Figure 3.9. Here, value labels can be added by simply completing the prompts for **Val<u>u</u>e**, **Val<u>u</u>e Label**, and using the push button **<u>A</u>dd**. Then, click **OK** to return to the **Variable View**. When the labels option is turned on as described above, the value labels appear in place of the numeric values.

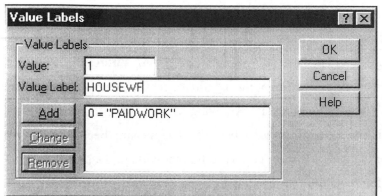

Figure 3.9   **Value Labels** dialog box, partially completed.

Additionally, in your output, you may wish to see descriptive labels for short variable names (SPSS allows only eight letters maximum to name a variable in the data set). For example, for the variable TIMEDRS, you may desire to have your output display and print the more descriptive label "Visits to Health Professionals." This feature is also executed in the **Variable View** by double clicking on the cell of the intersection between the **Labels** column and the variable of your choice. Once selected, simply type in the desired label, and click **OK** to return to the **Variable View**. Output 3.1 shows descriptive statistics for the variable TIMEDRS with the more complete label (e.g., "Visits to Health Professionals") shown.

Output 3.1 SPSS FREQUENCIES OUTPUT SHOWING DESCRIPTIVE LABELS.

Descriptive Statistics

	N	Minimum	Maximum	Mean	Std. Deviation
Visits to health professionals	461	0	81	7.92	10.99
Valid N (listwise)	461				

SPSS also defines missing values in the **Variable View**. Again, click on the cell of the intersection for the column **Missing** and the particular variable you are interested in, and then click the shaded ellipses in that cell. This action brings up the **Missing Values** dialog box, shown in Figure 3.10. The radio button for **Discrete Missing Values** defines specified data values or missing values as those values you wish to exclude from analysis. Knowing why a value is missing is often useful information. For example, you might want to distinguish between data missing because a subject failed to respond and data missing because the question didn't apply to that individual. Data values specified here as user-missing are flagged for special treatment and are excluded from most calculations. How a researcher wishes to treat missing values in a data set (e.g., replacing with the mean, etc.), is demonstrated in Chapter 4, in Section 4.1.3.

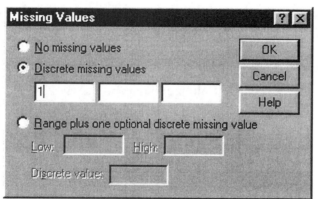

Figure 3.10   **Missing Values** dialog box.

Chapter 4. Cleaning Up Your Act: Screening Data Prior to Analysis

This chapter illustrates procedures in SPSS for screening ungrouped as well as grouped data with the complete example of Chapter 4 of *Using Multivariate Statistics*. To follow the example, use the data set titled SCREEN.sav, which can be obtained from the Internet site for this workbook. (See Section 3.1 of Chapter 3 for detailed information on obtaining the SPSS files.)

The first example evaluates distributions and relationships among six variables that are considered continuous in various multivariate analyses, such as multiple regression, canonical correlation, and factor analysis. These variables are: attitudes toward use of medication (ATTDRUG), attitude towards housework (ATTHOUSE), income (INCOME), current marital status (MSTATUS), race (RACE), and visits to health care professionals (TIMEDRS). The names of the variables are abbreviated because SPSS permits a maximum of eight characters (alpha or numeric) as a variable's name.

The second example looks at distributions and relationships among the six variables separately by groups formed by current employment status (EMPLMNT). The six variables are considered continuous in such multivariate procedures as multivariate analysis of covariance and discriminant function analysis.

4.1 SCREENING UNGROUPED DATA

4.1.1 Frequencies and Histograms for Initial Screening

The first run displays frequency distributions. Choose the following SPSS options, which are also displayed in Figures 4.1, 4.2 and 4.3.

```
>Analyze
    >Descriptive Statistics
        >Frequencies
            Variable(s)
                •attdrug
                •atthouse
                •income
                •mstatus
                •race
                •timedrs
            Charts . . .
                ⊙Histogram(s)
                    ☑With normal curve
            Statistics . . .
                Central Tendency: ☑all
                Dispersion: ☑all
                Distribution: ☑all
```

in the left pane you also can hide or display individual items, or collapse all the items under one or more headings. You can also drag items within the outline, move items up or down, or insert new items. Choose **Toolbar**, then **Outline Size**, then **Outline Font** from the **View** menu to access tools for manipulating the outline. Finally, you can pop up a helpful description of most elements in a pane by pointing the mouse arrow toward an icon or part of the pane of interest and clicking the right mouse button. This brings up a **What's this?** query. Simply click on it and a description appears.

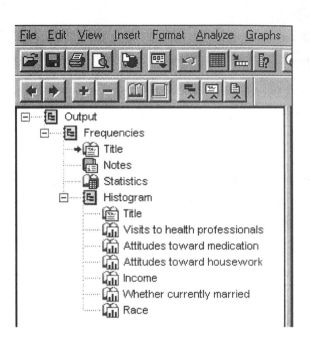

Figure 4.4   **Outline view** (left pane) of **Viewer** window.

The right pane in the **Viewer** window shows the results of your menu (or later on, syntax) selections. This pane contains statistical tables, charts, text, and other pertinent output. You navigate within this pane by using the horizontal and vertical scroll bars. You can also navigate in the right pane by jumping to a given object (e.g., table, chart). To do this, simply click on the desired object icon in the left pane and the right pane automatically jumps to the corresponding object.

Importantly, you can format the objects of your output in myriad ways, such as changing fonts, adding titles or legends, pivoting columns and rows, placing them in APA style, and much more. Further, you can paste and export your results into other applications, such as a word processing document (e.g., Word, WordPerfect), a page layout program (e.g., PageMaker, Quark), or a graphics program (e.g., PowerPoint, Photodraw, Illustrator, Freehand). For instruction on how to do this, consult the SPSS Tutorial, Help file, or many SPSS manuals, especially *SPSS Tables*. Briefly, click once on an object to select it (from here you can copy it to the clipboard). Double-click to activate an object for editing. If the object is a pivot table, you can obtain detailed help on items within the table by right-clicking on row and column labels after the table is activated. If the object is a chart, the double-click activates a **Chart Editor** window with its own menu and toolbar.

The statistics for the variables in the example are displayed in *Output 4.1*, below (see Table 4.5 in *UMS* for the accompanying histograms). Notice that the statistics for all of the variables are reported in one table. If you produce statistics tables for multiple variables, you can either display all variables in a single table (**Compare variables**) or display a separate statistics table for each variable (**Organize output by variables**). To access this option, click the **Format...** button from within the **Frequencies** dialog box (cf. Figure 4.1).

Output 4.1 **SPSS FREQUENCIES OUTPUT SHOWING DESCRIPTIVE STATISTICS FOR UNGROUPED DATA.**

Statistics

		Visits to health professionals	Attitudes toward medication	Attitudes toward housework	INCOME	Whether currently married	RACE
N	Valid	465	465	464	439	465	465
	Missing	0	0	1	26	0	0
Mean		7.90	7.69	23.54	4.21	1.78	1.09
Std. Error of Mean		.51	5.36E-02	.21	.12	1.93E-02	1.32E-02
Median		4.00	8.00	24.00	4.00	2.00	1.00
Mode		2	8	23	4	2	1
Std. Deviation		10.95	1.16	4.48	2.42	.42	.28
Variance		119.87	1.34	20.10	5.85	.17	8.06E-02
Skewness		3.248	-.123	-.457	.582	-1.346	2.914
Std. Error of Skewness		.113	.113	.113	.117	.113	.113
Kurtosis		13.101	-.447	1.556	-.359	-.190	6.521
Std. Error of Kurtosis		.226	.226	.226	.233	.226	.226
Range		81	5	33	9	1	1
Minimum		0	5	2	1	1	1
Maximum		81	10	35	10	2	2
Sum		3674	3574	10923	1848	827	506

SPSS offers numerous help facilities to assist with interpreting data. In addition to the **Help** menu under the main menu, there is the **Results Coach**. To access this help facility, right click on an output object, such as a table. This brings up a menu offering a number of useful utilities. One of the choices is the **Results Coach**. This SPSS generic tutorial provides elementary interpretation of many SPSS tables. Caution is advised, however, to not rely upon the **Results Coach** for complete interpretation of a particular statistic since only a generic description is provided and it does not address your data.

4.1.2 Frequencies and Histograms with Outliers Deleted

Table 4.5 in *UMS* shows the univariate outliers with very low scores on the variable Attitudes towards housework (ATTHOUSE). *Output 4.1* shows the minimum value to be 2, and that one value in the data set is missing. To delete outliers on a variable that has missing values, "undeclaring" the missing value code, at least temporarily, avoids deletion of the case with the missing value along with the outliers. Section 3.2 of this workbook shows dialog boxes managing missing values. To delete outliers for a given variable, follow these commands.

>D̲ata
　>Select C̲ases . . .
　　⊙If c̲ondition is satisfied
　　　"atthouse ne 2"

In this procedure, from the **D̲ata** menu, choose **Select C̲ases . . .** , which causes the **Select C̲ases** dialog box to pop up. Within this dialog box, click the radio button **I̲f condition is satisfied** and the push button **If . . .** . These steps activate the next pop-up dialog box, **Select Cases: If**. This box is shown in Figure 4.5.

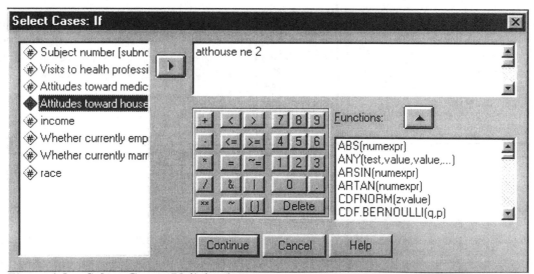

Figure 4.5　**Select Cases: If** dialog box.

20

Type the selection criterion, ATTHOUSE ne 2, in the box. (Note: "ne" means numeric "not equal to." Alternatively, the symbols "<>" may be used. The keypad notation "~=" is reserved for logical "not true" statements, rather than with numeric solutions.) Click the **Continue** button, and then the **OK** button in the main **Select Cases** dialog box. Also, click the radio button at the bottom of the window to delete the selected cases. The outliers are now deleted. Note that if you re-save the data file now, the outlying cases are permanently deleted from the data file so you might want to save the file using a different name to preserve your original data set. At this point you have 463 cases in the file, including the one with a missing value on ATTHOUSE. Re-declare the missing value on ATTHOUSE (Section 3.2) before continuing.

An alternative procedure for deleting a case is to go directly into the data file, by clicking anywhere in the data file window. Then, click on the case number (leftmost, permanently bolded and gray-shaded column in the spreadsheet, cf. Figure 3.6), and delete the case by choosing these commands:

>Edit
    >Clear

Yet another alternative is to create a new variable (e.g., OUTLIER, using the **Compute** menu) that is defined to not contain the outliers you specify. Specify that all values in the new variable are 0. Next, manually change the outliers from 0 to 1 in the data set. Finally, select just the cases in OUTLIER that are less than 1.

>Data
    >Select Cases . . .
        ⊙ If condition is satisfied
            OUTLIER <1

Once the outliers are deleted by whatever method, the **Frequencies** dialog boxes (cf. Figures 4.1, 4.2, and 4.3) are used to produce the frequencies and histogram for ATTHOUSE with univariate outliers deleted (see Table 4.6 in *UMS*).

4.1.3 Replacing a Missing Value with the Mean

You will note in in *Output 4.1* of this workbook that one case for ATTHOUSE is missing. Replacing the missing ATTHOUSE value with the mean is accomplished through the SPSS commands given below. After the single value has been recoded, the frequency output will match that of Table 4.5 in *UMS*.

```
>Transform
    >Recode
        Into Same Variable . . .
            Variables:
                •atthouse
            Old and New Values...
                Old Value
                    ⊙System-missing
                New Value
                    ⊙Value = 23.634
```

The **Recode into Same Variables** dialog box is shown in Figure 4.6. Access this from the **Transform** and then **Recode**, and **Into Same Variables ...** menu choices.

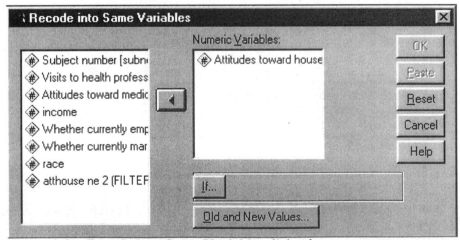

Figure 4.6   **Recode into Same Variables** dialog box.

From here, move the variable Attitudes Towards Housework (viz., ATTHOUSE) into the **Numeric Variables** box by highlighting it and clicking the right arrow. Then, use the push button **Old** and New Values ..... . This action brings up the **Recode into Same Variables: Old and New Values** dialog box, shown in Figure 4.7. In the **Old Value** part of the dialog box, click on the **System missing** radio button; and, in the **New Value** part of the dialog box, click the **Value** radio button and type into the text box the mean for ATTHOUSE, 23.63. (Of course, the value 23.634 is known from the mean of the variable ATTHOUSE, as shown in Table 4.6 of *UMS*.) To move the new value into the active **Old -->New:** box, click the **Add** push button.

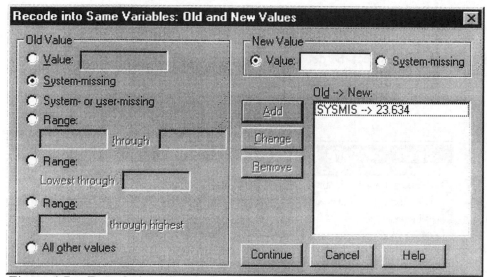

Figure 4.7   **Recode into Same Variables: Old and New Values** dialog box.

4.1.4 Plots for Linearity and Homoscedasticity

Scatterplots for checking these assumptions can be accessed through the following SPSS commands.

```
>Graphs
    >Scatter . . .
            Simple
            Define
                    Y Axis:
                            •timedrs
                    X Axis:
                            •attdrug
```

The **Scatterplot** dialog box is shown in Figure 4.8. **Simple** is the default; leave it highlighted.

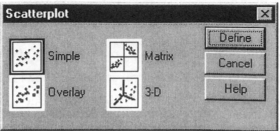
Figure 4.8   **Scatterplot** dialog box.

Use the **Define** push button, which activates the **Simple Scatterplot** dialog box, shown in Figure 4.9. Within this dialog box, select the dependent variable (TIMEDRS) for the **Y Axis:** and the independent variable (ATTDRUG) for the **X Axis:**. Complete the procedure by clicking **OK**.

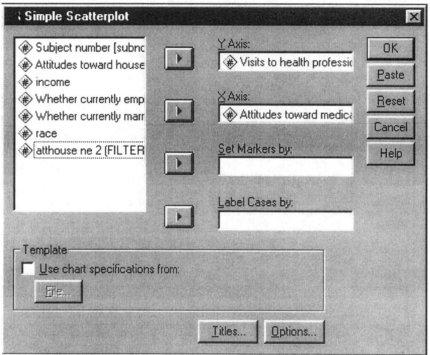
Figure 4.9   **Simple Scatterplot** dialog box.

This produces Figure 4.9 of *UMS*, which shows that both nonlinearity and heteroscedasticity exist between variables.

4.1.5 Transformation

The transformation of TIMEDRS to improve normality, linearity, and homoscedasticity is accomplished by the following SPSS commands.

```
>Transform...
    >Compute . . .
        Target Variable: ltimedrs
        Functions: LG10(numexpr)
        Numeric Expression:
            LG10(timedrs + 1)
```

The **Compute Variable** dialog box is show in Figure 4.10, and the procedure is described in *UMS*.

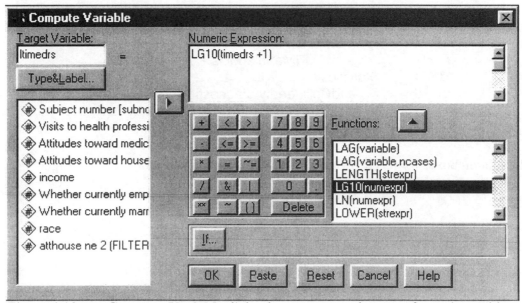

Figure 4.10   **Compute Variable** dialog box to create a log-transformed variable.

When frequency statistics and histograms are requested for the newly created variable (LTIMEDRS), new statistics tables and histograms are produced, as displayed in Table 4.7 of *UMS*..

4.1.6 Detecting Multivariate Outliers through Regression

Multivariate outliers are detected through the centroid-distance statistic Mahalanobis, which is accessed in SPSS through the regression procedure. (Regression procedures are discussed in Chapter 5 of *UMS*.) Follow these commands.

```
>Analyze
    >Regression
        >Linear
            Dependent:
                •subno
            Independent(s)
                •attdrug
                •atthouse
                •mstatus
                •race
                •ltimedrs
            Save . . .
                Distances
                    ☑Mahalanobis
            Statistics
                ☑Collinearity diagnostics
```

The dialog boxes for this regression procedure noted above are displayed in Figures 4.11 to 4.13.

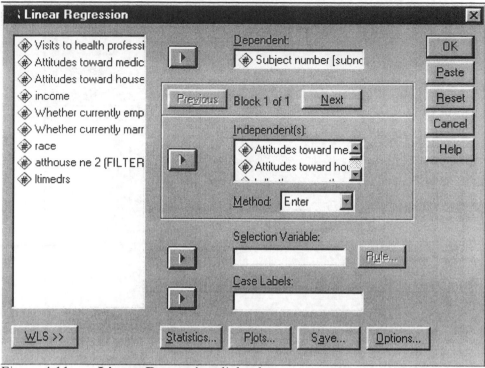

Figure 4.11   **Linear Regression** dialog box.

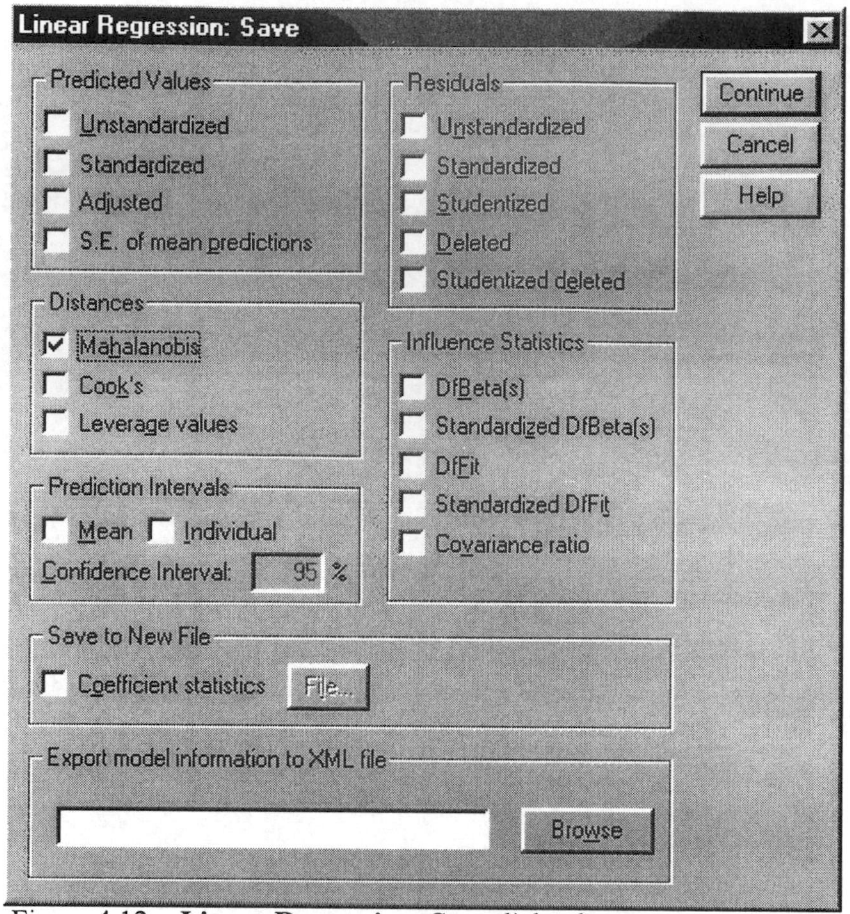

Figure 4.12   **Linear Regression: Save** dialog box.

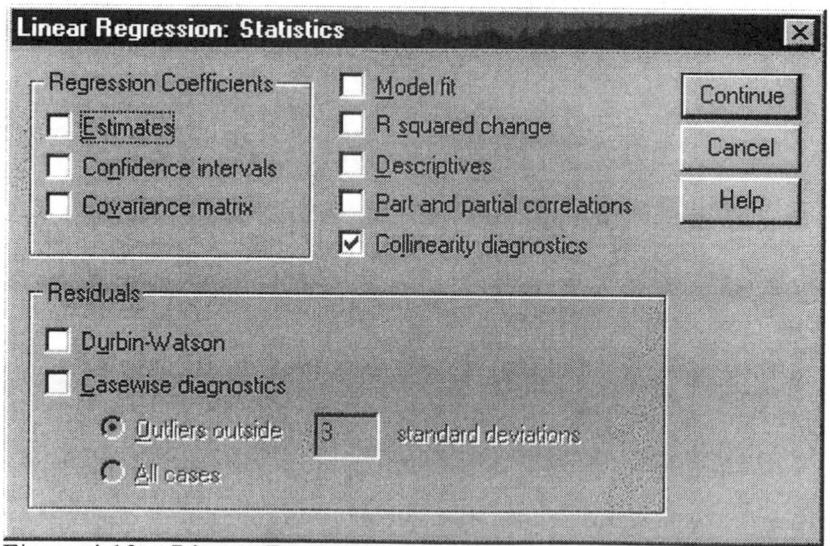

Figure 4.13   **Linear Regression: Statistics** dialog box for
collinearity diagnostics.

The procedure produces a new variable in your data set of the Mahalanobis distance, called "mah_1". Figure 4.14 displays a portion of the data set in the **Data Editor** view showing the creation of the new variable. Now, the data set can be scanned for multivariate outliers by looking for values that exceed the Mahalanobis critical value of 20.515 for $\alpha = .001$ with five variables, as discussed in Section 4.2.1.4 of *UMS*.

	subno	timedrs	attdrug	atthouse	income	emplmnt	mstatus	race	ltimedrs	mah_1
114	134	4	9	26	3	HOUSEWF	2	1	.70	2.06794
115	135	4	8	21	3	HOUSEWF	2	1	.70	.80984
116	136	6	7	18	8	PAIDWORK	2	1	.85	2.60890
117	137	30	5	24	10	PAIDWORK	2	2	1.49	21.83684
118	138	7	8	28	99	HOUSEWF	1	1	.90	4.55610
119	139	15	7	26	1	HOUSEWF	2	1	1.20	2.31735
120	140	6	7	25	8	HOUSEWF	2	2	.85	11.66335

Figure 4.14   **Data Editor** window showing newly created variable: Mahalanobis distance ("mah_1").

4.1.7 Variables Causing Cases to be Outliers

Stepwise regression is used to discover which combination of variables causes cases to be multivariate outliers. First a dummy variable with all cases set to "0" (to be used as the DV) is created by following the SPSS commands below.

```
>Transform
    >Compute . . .
        Target Variable: dummy
        Numeric Expression: 0
```

Figure 4.15 shows the **Compute Variable** dialog box for this procedure.

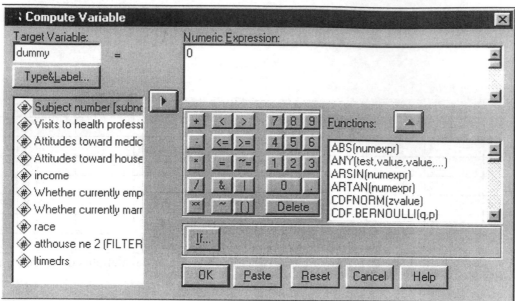

Figure 4.15   **Compute Variable** dialog box to create dummy variable

Go to case 117, the case in the mah_1 variable whose value exceeds the critical value. For case 117, change DUMMY to "1". (Chapter 13 shows an alternative way to change the code of DUMMY to 1 when you have many outliers.) Next, follow the regression procedure. The SPSS commands are given below.

```
>Analyze
    >Regression
        >Linear
            Dependent:
                •dummy
            Independent(s)
                •attdrug
                •atthouse
                •mstatus
                •race
                •ltimedrs
            Method: = stepwise
```

Remember to undo previous selections in this dialog that are no longer needed. Click the **Statistics**... button, uncheck **Collinearity diagnostics**, and check **Estimates** and **Model fit**; also, click the **Save**... button and uncheck the **Mahalanobis** option. Some of the output from this run is displayed in Table 4.9 of *UMS*. From here you can consult Table 4.5 of *UMS* to find the mean values on ATTDRUG, LTIMEDRS and RACE against which to compare the values for case 117.

The other multivariate outlier is Case 193. To diagnosis this outlier, change the value in the data set for case 193 to "1" and reset the value for case 117 back to "0". Another stepwise regression run then identifies the variables causing the 193rd case to be an outlier.

4.1.8 Multicollinearity

The Linear Regression run of Section 4.1.6 to detect multivariate outliers is also used to produce collinearity diagnostics. Table 4.8 of *UMS* shows the output.

4.2 SCREENING GROUPED DATA

The procedures for screening grouped data are similar to those of ungrouped data, with the exception that each group is analyzed separately. Follow the SPSS commands below to split the file for separate analysis. Note that two options are available to view split-file analysis. When the **Compare groups** option is selected, the split-file groups are presented together for comparison purposes. When **Organize output by groups** is selected, results from each procedure are displayed separately for each split-file group. The following commands produce Figure 4.16.

>Data
   >Split File . . .
      ⊙Organize output by groups
         Groups Based on
           •emplmnt

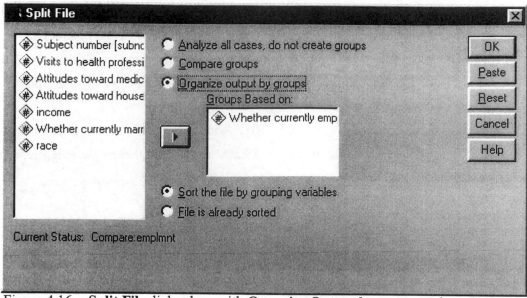

Figure 4.16   **Split File** dialog box with **<u>O</u>rganize Output by groups** selected.

4.2.1 Frequencies and Histograms

Requesting frequencies and histograms is identical to that for ungrouped data (cf. Section 4.1.1); that is, procedures shown in Figures 4.1 through 4.3 are followed. *Output 4.2* shows TIMEDRS frequencies and histograms for the two groups.

Output 4.2 **FREQUENCIES FOR TIMEDRS, SEPARATELY FOR EACH EMPLMNT GROUP**

EMPLMNT = PAIDWORK

Statistics[a]

Visits to health professionals

N	Valid	246
	Missing	0
Mean		7.29
Std. Error of Mean		.71
Median		4.00
Mode		2
Std. Deviation		11.07
Variance		122.45
Skewness		3.872
Std. Error of Skewness		.155
Kurtosis		18.077
Std. Error of Kurtosis		.309
Range		81
Minimum		0
Maximum		81
Sum		1794

a. EMPLMNT = PAIDWORK

EMPLMNT = HOUSEWFE

Statistics^a

Visits to health professionals

N	Valid	219
	Missing	0
Mean		8.58
Std. Error of Mean		.73
Median		4.00
Mode		2
Std. Deviation		10.80
Variance		116.63
Skewness		2.562
Std. Error of Skewness		.164
Kurtosis		7.865
Std. Error of Kurtosis		.327
Range		60
Minimum		0
Maximum		60
Sum		1880

a. EMPLMNT = HOUSEWFE

Visits to health professionals

EMPLMNT: 0   PAIDWORK

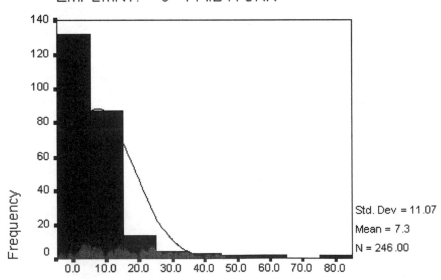

Std. Dev = 11.07
Mean = 7.3
N = 246.00

Visits to health professionals

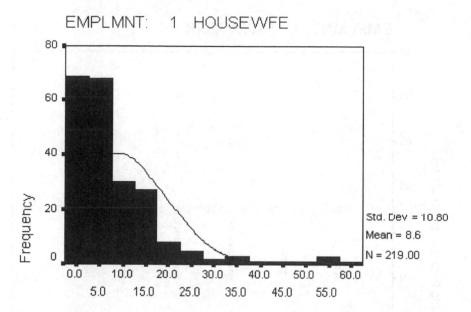

EMPLMNT: 1 HOUSEWFE

Std. Dev = 10.60
Mean = 8.6
N = 219.00

4.2.2 Scatterplots for Linearity

The procedure for producing scatterplots for grouped data is the same as for ungrouped data (Section 4.1.4) once the analysis is specified by groups (cf. Section 4.2). *Output 4.3* which shows the ATTDRUG by TIMEDRS scatterplots for the two employment groups.

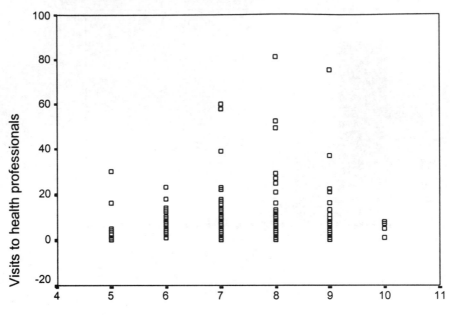

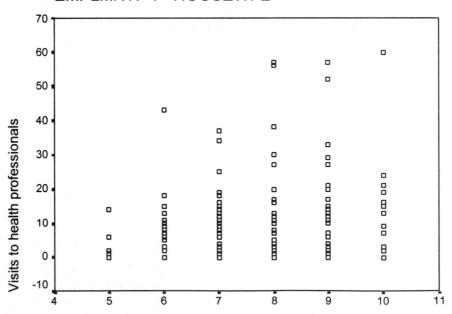

4.2.3 Multivariate Outliers and Multicollinearity

SPSS has no provision for detecting within-group outliers. The procedure can be approximated by separate regression analyses for each of the EMPLMNT groups. (Note that the multiple DVs in analyses with grouped data, such as MANOVA, are treated as IVs in multiple regression for purposes of finding outliers among cases.) A request for multiple regression (as per Section 4.1.6) with the **Split File** turned on (cf. Figure 4.16) produces separate regressions for each group, with Mahalanobis distance for each case saved to the data file.

However, Mahalanobis distance produced by separate regressions for each group will be somewhat different from within-group Mahalanobis distance, due to differences in the algorithms for the two methods. Therefore, different cases may be detected as multivariate outliers than are identified in Section 4.2.2.3 of *UMS*.

Transformation of TIMEDRS (Section 4.1.5) proceeds as with ungrouped data (Sections 4.1.5). Identification of multivariate outliers through separate regressions for each group should follow, with TIMEDRS replaced by LTIMEDRS. Then, identification of variables causing outliers through stepwise regression proceeds as in Section 4.1.7. The separate regressions for each group can also be used to check for multicollinearity by requesting collinearity diagnostics, as per Section 4.1.6.

Chapter 5. Multiple Regression

This chapter demonstrates two multiple regression techniques: standard and sequential ordering of variables. Following the evaluation of appropriate assumptions, the techniques are explained and illustrated with the complete example of Chapter 5 of *Using Multivariate Statistics*. The SPSS data file used in this chapter is REGRESS.sav, which can be obtained from the Internet site for this workbook. (See Section 3.1 of Chapter 3 for detailed information on obtaining the SPSS files.)

The first example employs standard multiple regression to evaluate the prediction of visits to health professionals by physical and mental health symptoms and stress associated with major life changes. The second example takes a sequential approach to regression with the same predictors. This time the variables are cumulatively ordered, first as visits to health professionals with physical health symptoms alone, next with the addition of life change stress, and finally with the further addition of mental health symptoms. The point of such sequential addition of variables is to evaluate whether adding specific variables, in a given order, contributes to prediction beyond that available from prior variables.

5.1   EVALUATION OF ASSUMPTIONS

Frequencies, histograms, and transformations are demonstrated in Sections 4.1.1, 4.1.2, and 4.1.5. Detection of outliers through Mahalanobis distance using multiple regression is demonstrated in Section 4.1.6.

It is typical to begin evaluating assumptions used in multiple regression by examining scatterplots of residuals. SPSS allows for producing scatterplots from within the **Regression Plots ...** command. Follow these SPSS commands.

```
>Analyze
      >Regression
            >Linear
                  Dependent:
                        •timedrs
                  Independent(s)
                        •menheal
                        •phyheal
                        •stress
                  Plots . . .
                        Y: = *zresid
                        X: = *zpred
```

Figure 5.1 shows the main regression dialog box. Enter the variables as shown. Then click the **Plots...** push button to activate the **Linear Regression: Plots** dialog box and add the values for the **X** and **Y** axes as shown in Figure 5.2. Then, click **Continue** to return to the main **Linear Regression** dialog box. Once back in the main dialog box click **OK** and the regression output is produced. While the output is for the full regression, our current interest is in the scatterplot. Navigate through the output to the scatterplot by clicking in the left pane on the last element—the scatterplot icon followed by the title *zpred by *zresid scatterplot. This left pane is illustrated in Figure 5.3. Notice that the right pane jumps to the scatterplot, which is shown in Figure 5.4, which duplicates Figure 5.5 in *UMS*.

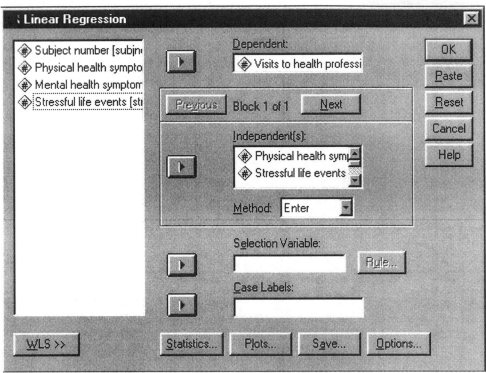

Figure 5.1 **Linear Regression** dialog box for residuals.

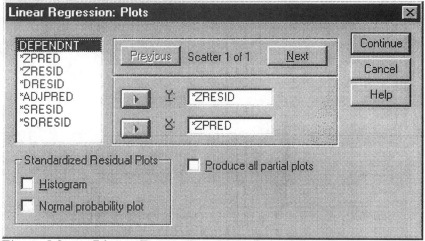

Figure 5.2   **Linear Regression: Plots** dialog box.

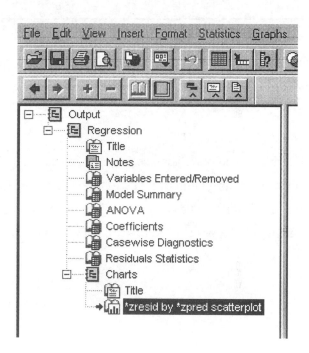

Figure 5.3   Left pane window to navigate
                to scatterplot.

Scatterplot

Dependent Variable: Visits to health professionals

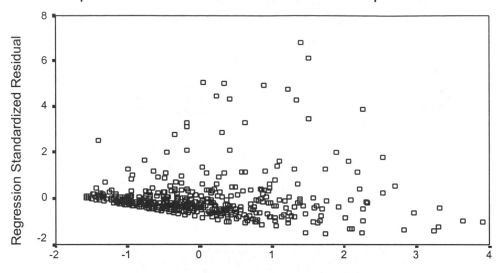

Figure 5.4   Standardized residual scatterplot for original variables

Through examining scatterplots (and other analyses, e.g., skewness, kurtosis) we see the need for transformation of several variables. Transformation of LTIMEDRS, which appears in the variable list of Figure 5.5, was demonstrated in Section 4.1.5. The square root transformation of STRESS, renamed into the target variable SSTRESS, is shown in Figure 5.5. Similarly, PHYHEAL is log-transformed into LPHYHEAL.

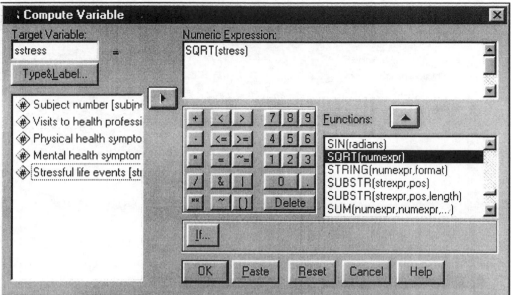

Figure 5.5 **Compute Variable** dialog box to produce SSTRESS.

Now, we can recheck the assumptions with the newly-transformed variables. To do this, use the procedures as illustrated above for checking assumptions and producing scatterplots, only replace the variables which were transformed by their corollaries in the variables list boxes for DV and IVs. Figure 5.6 shows the main dialog box for this procedure. (Notice that this box was used previously and illustrated in Figure 5.1. Here, the transformed variables are entered.)

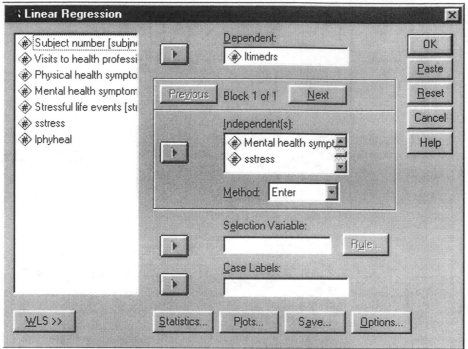

Figure 5.6   **Linear Regression** dialog box for transformed variables.

Figure 5.7 show the scatterplot for ltimedrs, employing the procedures illustrated above. Contrast this scatterplot to that shown in Figure 5.4, the same variable before transformation.

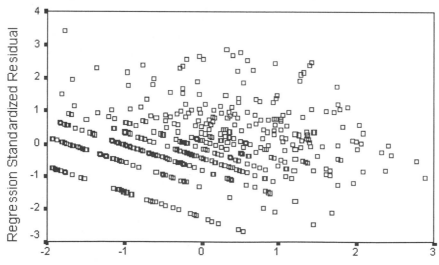

Figure 5.7   Standardized residuals scatterplot of transformed variables

After screening the data and checking the assumptions, we are at last ready to run the multiple regression procedure. Remember to use the transformed variables for this analysis.

Multicollinearity information is available in the main analysis that follows.

5.2   STANDARD MULTIPLE REGRESSION

The commands listed above and illustrated in Figure 5.6 produce standard multiple regression. Clicking on the **Statistics...** button in the **Linear Regression** dialog box allows you to choose additional output, such as **Confidence intervals**, **Descriptives**, **Part and partial correlations**, and **Collinearity diagnostics**. These procedures are cited below and shown in Figure 5.8.

```
>Analyze
    >Regression
        >Linear
            Dependent:
                •ltimedrs
            Independent(s)
                •menheal
                •lphyheal
                •sstress
            Statistics . . .
                ☑Confidence intervals
                ☑Descriptives
                ☑Part and partial correlations
                ☑Collinearity diagnostics
            Residuals
                ☑Durbin-Watson
                ☑Casewise diagnostics
```

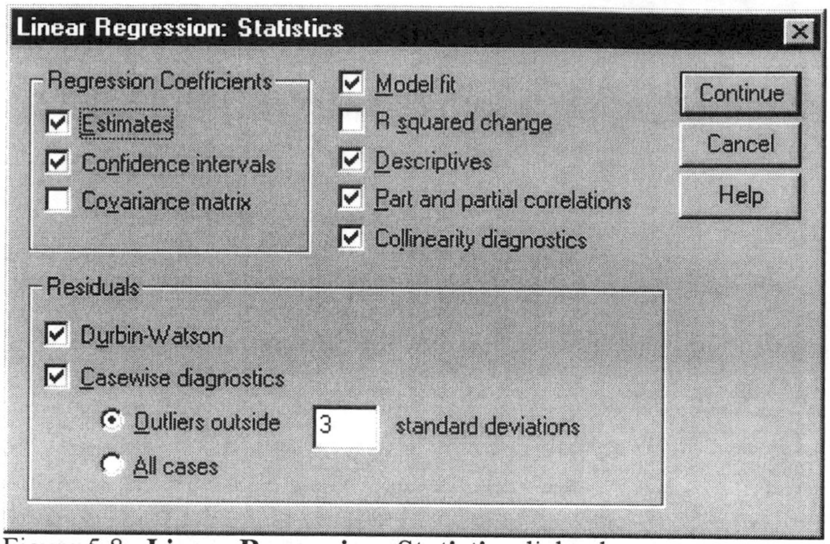

Figure 5.8 **Linear Regression: Statistics** dialog box.

You may opt to go back into the **Linear Regression: Plots** dialog box (cf. Figures 5.1 and 5.2) and deselect the plots to simplify your output. The output produced matches that of Tables 5.15 and 5.16 in *UMS*, and is not repeated here.

5.3   SEQUENTIAL REGRESSION

Sequential ordering of variables for regression is run similarly to standard regression except that the variables are not entered simultaneously; rather, they are entered into the equation in a specified sequence, to see their relative contribution to the solution. As before, first choose the SPSS linear regression procedures shown below and illustrated in Figures 5.9 to 5.11. Notice particularly that the variables enter the equation one at a time, differentiated by Block 1, Block 2, and Block 3. To do this, add just one variable to the variables list box (cf. Figure 5.9), then click the **Next** button, which automatically clears the list box and moves to Block 2. Again, enter just one variable (cf. Figure 5.10), and click the **Next** button to move to Block 3. Enter the third and final variable (cf. Figure 5.11).

>Analyze
>Regression
>Linear
Dependent:
•ltimedrs
Block 1 of 1
Independent(s)
•lphyheal
Next
Block 2 of 2
•sstress
Next
Block 3 of 3
•menheal
Plots . . .
Y: = *zresid
X: = *zpred

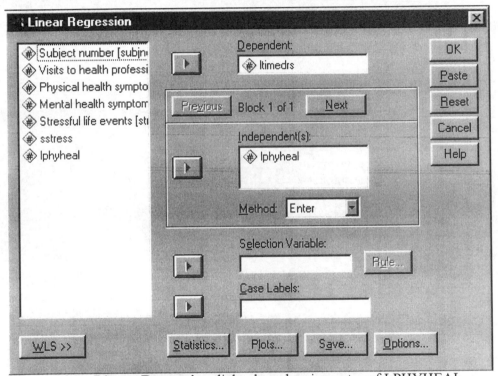

Figure 5.9   **Linear Regression** dialog box showing entry of LPHYHEAL,
the first IV.

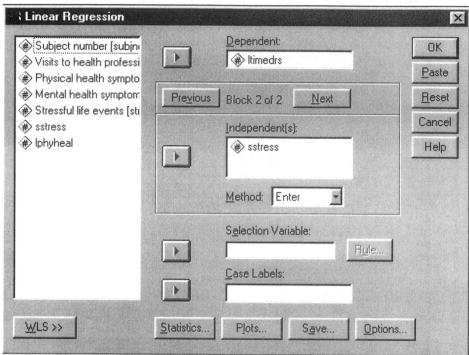

Figure 5.10   **Linear Regression** dialog box showing entry of SSTRESS, the second IV.

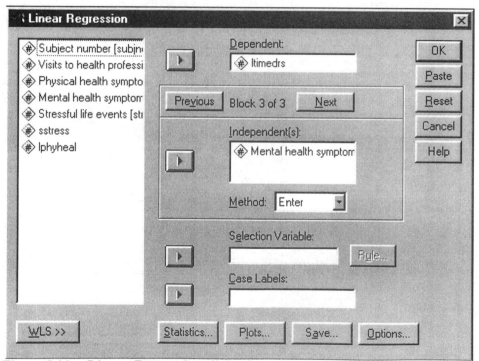

Figure 5.11   **Linear Regression** dialog box showing entry of MENHEAL, the last IV.

The output matches Table 5.19 of *UMS*. Of particular interest is the Model Summary and the Coefficients, which are displayed. Navigate to the portions of the output that contain these tables by clicking on the appropriate element in the left pane of the SPSS Viewer window (i.e., "Model Summary" and "Coefficients").

Chapter 6. Canonical Correlation

This chapter demonstrates procedures for canonical correlation with SPSS for the complete example of Chapter 6 of *Using Multivariate Statistics*. To follow the example, use the data set titled CANON.sav, which can be obtained from the Internet site for this workbook. (See Section 3.1 of Chapter 3 for detailed information on obtaining the SPSS files.)

The example examines relationships between a set of attitudinal variables and another set of health variables. The attitudinal variables are attitudes toward the role of women (ATTROLE), locus of control (CONTROL), attitudes toward marital status (ATTMAR), and self-esteem (ESTEEM). The health variables are mental health symptoms (MENHEAL), physical health symptoms (PHYHEAL), visits to health professionals (TIMEDRS), attitudes toward use of medication (ATTDRUG), and use of psychotropic drugs (DRUGUSE).

6.1 EVALUATION OF ASSUMPTIONS

Tests for normality, linearity, and homoscedasticity for individual variables proceed as described in Chapter 4 (cf. Sections 4.1.1, 4.1.2). In Chapter 6 of *UMS*, the need for log transformation of three of the health variables (TIMEDRS, PHYHEAL, and DRUGUSE) and one of the attitudinal variables (ATTMAR) is explained. Procedures to transform these variables to produce LTIMEDRS, LPHYHEAL, LDRUGUSE, and LATTMAR are described in Section 4.1.5.

Identifying and interpreting multivariate outliers is accomplished separately for each set of variables respectively, using the multiple regression procedures explained in Section 4.1.6. Note that the six cases with data missing on locus of control (CONTROL) or ATTMAR need to be deleted from both multiple regression runs to search for multivariate outliers.

SPSS assesses collinearity in the regression procedures (**Statistics: Collinearity diagnostics**), considering all such ANOVA statistics to be part of a general linear model. However, these procedures are complicated because in canonical correlation there is a canonical set of variables on each side of the equation. Thus, collinearity diagnostics require separate ANALYSIS and DESIGN statements for each set of variables. Further, when indications of difficulty are revealed in such diagnosis, additional analysis is required. Hence, a simpler diagnosis through factor analysis (cf. Chapter 13 of *UMS*) is shown here[1]. Factor analysis is run separately on each set of variables to examine SMCs (squared multiple

---

[1] Factor analysis is discussed in Chapter 13. The technique is used here simply for its production of diagnostic information for canonical analysis.

correlations), identified as initial communalities in principal factor analysis). Follow these SPSS procedures to execute this diagnostic analysis. Figures 6.1 and 6.2 illustrate the steps.

>Analyze
    >Data Reduction
        >Factor . . .
            Variables:
                •esteem
                •control
                •lattmar
                •attrole
            Extraction...
                Method = Principal axis factoring

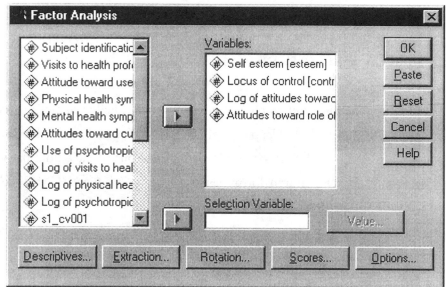

Figure 6.1   **Factor Analysis** dialog box for first set of variables.

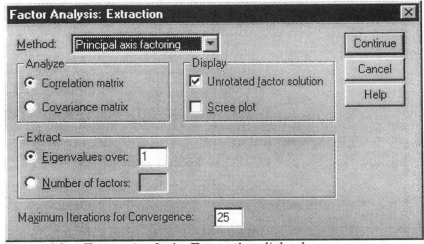

Figure 6.2   **Factor Analysis: Extraction** dialog box.

The output for this procedure is shown in *Output 6.1*.

Output 6.1 **FACTOR ANALYSIS ON FIRST SET OF VARIABLES TO CHECK FOR MULTICOLLINEARITY. PARTIAL OUTPUT.**

Communalities

	Initial	Extraction
Self esteem	.227	.705
Locus of control	.133	.197
Log of attitudes toward current marital status	.132	.252
Attitudes toward role of women	6.751E-02	.343

Extraction Method: Principal Axis Factoring.

Total Variance Explained

Factor	Initial Eigenvalues			Extraction Sums of Squared Loadings		
	Total	% of Variance	Cumulative %	Total	% of Variance	Cumulative %
1	1.587	39.665	39.665	1.069	26.715	26.715
2	1.093	27.313	66.978	.428	10.689	37.404
3	.777	19.430	86.408			
4	.544	13.592	100.000			

Extraction Method: Principal Axis Factoring.

Parallel procedures for the second set of variables (LTIMEDRS, ATTDRUG, LPHYHEAL, MENHEAL, and LDRUGUSE) are illustrated in Figure 6.3. These steps produce *Output 6.2.*

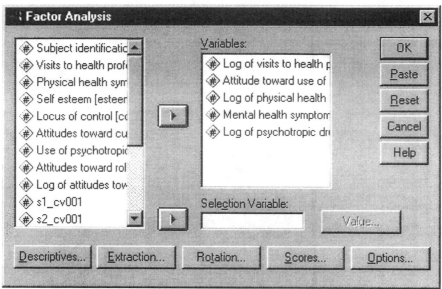

Figure 6.3   **Factor Analysis** dialog box for second set of variables

Output 6.2 **FACTOR ANALYSIS ON SECOND SET OF VARIABLES TO CHECK FOR MULTICOLLINEARITY. PARTIAL OUTPUT.**

Communalities

	Initial	Extraction
Log of visits to health professionals	.368	.422
Attitude toward use of drugs	8.095E-02	.140
Log of physical health symptoms	.473	.816
Mental health symptoms	.291	.328
Log of psychotropic drug use	.307	.643

Extraction Method: Principal Axis Factoring.

Total Variance Explained

Factor	Initial Eigenvalues			Extraction Sums of Squared Loadings		
	Total	% of Variance	Cumulative %	Total	% of Variance	Cumulative %
1	2.413	48.251	48.251	1.986	39.724	39.724
2	1.010	20.196	68.447	.362	7.241	46.965
3	.650	12.997	81.444			
4	.553	11.056	92.499			
5	.375	7.501	100.000			

Extraction Method: Principal Axis Factoring.

As can be seen in *Output 6.1* and *Output 6.2*, there is no threat of multicollinearity because the communalities (SMCs) do not approach 1.00.

6.2   CANONICAL CORRELATION

Because, in canonical correlation, canonical sets can be interchanged (and even variables within sets may be replaced), there is no distinction between DVs and IVs. For this reason SPSS opted to expunge canonical procedures from MANOVA where it was accessed in previous versions; instead, SPSS has assigned canonical correlation as a special macro (a separate, independent program).

The SPSS canonical correlation macro is accessed through the main SPSS help menu. From the main menu bar, click on **Help**, then **Topics**, and select the Index tab. Type in the first box, "canonical correlation macro," as illustrated in Figure 6.4. Then, click the **Display** button and the macro is revealed, as shown in Figure 6.5.

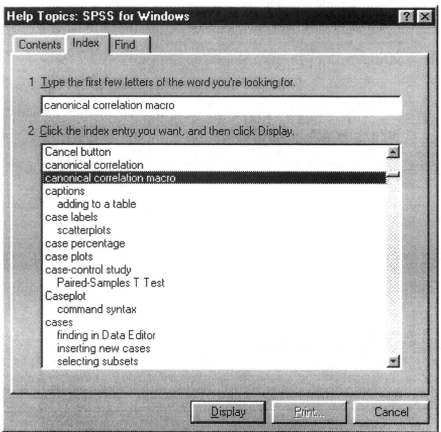

Figure 6.4   **Help Topics: SPSS for Windows** for finding canonical
correlation macro.

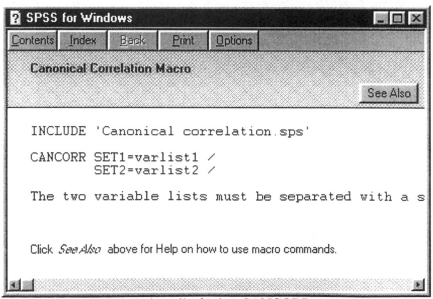

Figure 6.5   **Help** window displaying CANCORR macro.

Highlight the entire macro (omit the "Click *See Also...*" note at the bottom of the window) and copy it to the system clipboard (i.e., Ctrl C). At this point, open a new syntax box by following these SPSS commands.

F̲ile
>N̲ew
>S̲yntax

Now, simply paste the macro into the syntax box (Ctrl V). Within the syntax box, replace "varlist1" with the first canonical set (i.e., ESTEEM, CONTROL, LATTMAR, and ATTROLE) and "varlist2" with the second canonical set (LTIMEDRS, ATTDRUG, LPHYHEAL, MENHEAL, and LDRUGUSE). Be careful to not accidentally delete the slash (/) or the syntax terminator (.)—SPSS needs these codes! Figure 6.6 illustrates the completed syntax box. Your data file must also be open in the **Data Editor** window. Run the macro by either clicking on the **Run** button (right arrow on the toolbar) or selecting **Run**, **All** from the main menu. Note also that it is not a requirement that both sets have the same number of variables. The canonical output is illustrated in *Output 6.3*. Also notice that canonical scores have been automatically written by SPSS to the active data file. Such scores can be employed in further analysis.

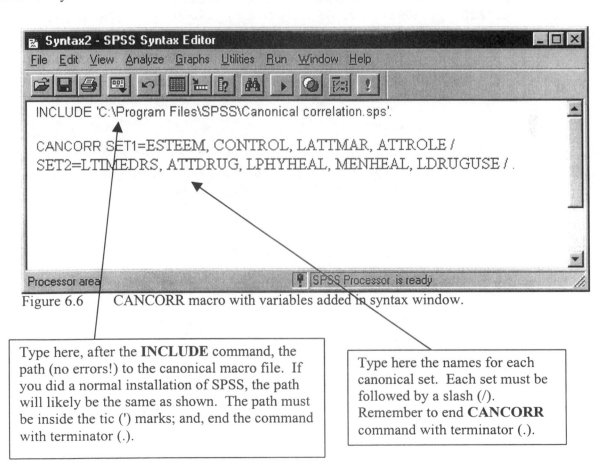

Figure 6.6   CANCORR macro with variables added in syntax window.

Type here, after the **INCLUDE** command, the path (no errors!) to the canonical macro file. If you did a normal installation of SPSS, the path will likely be the same as shown. The path must be inside the tic (') marks; and, end the command with terminator (.).

Type here the names for each canonical set. Each set must be followed by a slash (/). Remember to end **CANCORR** command with terminator (.).

Output 6.3 CANONICAL CORRELATION ANALYSIS OF ATTITUDINAL AND HEALTH
VARIABLES: PARTIAL OUTPUT

```
Correlations for Set-1
           ATTROLE  CONTROL  LATTMAR   ESTEEM
ATTROLE    1.0000    .0006   -.1017    .1903
CONTROL     .0006   1.0000    .2050    .3467
LATTMAR    -.1017    .2050   1.0000    .3106
 ESTEEM     .1903    .3467    .3106   1.0000


Correlations for Set-2
           MENHEAL  LPHYHEAL  LTIMEDRS  ATTDRUG  DRUGUSE
 MENHEAL   1.0000    .5122     .3620     .0665    .3901
LPHYHEAL    .5122   1.0000     .5871     .1151    .4297
LTIMEDRS    .3620    .5871    1.0000     .1054    .4190
 ATTDRUG    .0665    .1151     .1054    1.0000    .3083
 DRUGUSE    .3901    .4297     .4190     .3083   1.0000


Correlations Between Set-1 and Set-2
           MENHEAL  LPHYHEAL  LTIMEDRS  ATTDRUG  DRUGUSE
ATTROLE    -.0744   -.0608    -.1250     .1146   -.1012
CONTROL     .2859    .1194     .0407     .0534    .0681
LATTMAR     .2717    .0997     .0278    -.0335    .0938
 ESTEEM     .1991    .1085    -.0121     .1020   -.0408


      Canonical Correlations
      1      .381
      2      .255
      3      .094
      4      .039


      Test that remaining correlations are zero:
           Wilk's   Chi-SQ        DF      Sig.
      1      .791   106.050    20.000     .000
      2      .925    35.183    12.000     .000
      3      .990     4.665     6.000     .587
      4      .999      .675     2.000     .714
```

58

```
Standardized Canonical Coefficients for Set-1
                 1         2         3         4
ATTROLE       -.073     -.595     -.841     -.074
CONTROL        .582      .080     -.100     -.893
LATTMAR        .507      .435     -.621      .566
 ESTEEM        .279     -.671      .745      .459


Raw Canonical Coefficients for Set-1
                 1         2         3         4
ATTROLE       -.011     -.088     -.125     -.011
CONTROL        .458      .063     -.078     -.703
LATTMAR       3.288     2.821    -4.031     3.674
 ESTEEM        .071     -.170      .189      .116


Standardized Canonical Coefficients for Set-2
                 1         2         3         4
 MENHEAL      1.072      .027     -.164     -.108
LPHYHEAL       .061     -.412      .476      .741
LTIMEDRS      -.258      .372      .829     -.641
 ATTDRUG       .083     -.811      .002     -.654
 DRUGUSE      -.143      .785     -.599     -.298


Raw Canonical Coefficients for Set-2
                 1         2         3         4
 MENHEAL       .259      .007     -.040     -.026
LPHYHEAL       .295    -1.993     2.302     3.585
LTIMEDRS      -.619      .893     1.990    -1.538
 ATTDRUG       .072     -.703      .001     -.566
 DRUGUSE      -.014      .077     -.059     -.029


Canonical Loadings for Set-1
                 1         2         3         4
ATTROLE       -.072     -.767     -.636     -.045
CONTROL        .783     -.063      .031     -.618
LATTMAR        .720      .303     -.325      .533
 ESTEEM        .624     -.621      .358      .311


Cross Loadings for Set-1
                 1         2         3         4
ATTROLE       -.027     -.196     -.060     -.002
CONTROL        .298     -.016      .003     -.024
LATTMAR        .274      .077     -.030      .021
 ESTEEM        .237     -.159      .034      .012
```

```
Canonical Loadings for Set-2
                   1        2        3        4
     MENHEAL     .960     .203     .146    -.120
    LPHYHEAL     .407     .064     .621     .106
    LTIMEDRS     .115     .383     .798    -.439
     ATTDRUG     .090    -.575    -.052    -.735
     DRUGUSE     .219     .524    -.111    -.492


Cross Loadings for Set-2
                   1        2        3        4
     MENHEAL     .365     .052     .014    -.005
    LPHYHEAL     .155     .016     .058     .004
    LTIMEDRS     .044     .098     .075    -.017
     ATTDRUG     .034    -.147    -.005    -.028
     DRUGUSE     .083     .134    -.010    -.019


      Redundancy Analysis:



Proportion of Variance of Set-1 Explained by Its Own Can. Var.
               Prop Var
CV1-1            .381
CV1-2            .268
CV1-3            .160
CV1-4            .191


Proportion of Variance of Set-1 Explained by Opposite Can.Var.
               Prop Var
CV2-1            .055
CV2-2            .017
CV2-3            .001
CV2-4            .000


Proportion of Variance of Set-2 Explained by Its Own Can. Var.
               Prop Var
CV2-1            .231
CV2-2            .160
CV2-3            .212
CV2-4            .200


Proportion of Variance of Set-2 Explained by Opposite Can. Var.
               Prop Var
CV1-1            .033
CV1-2            .010
CV1-3            .002
CV1-4            .000

------ END MATRIX -----
```

60

The SPSS output begins with bivariate correlations among all the variables within and between each set. Canonical correlations are then shown, differing a bit from the SAS values in Section 6.6.2 of *UMS*. Squared canonical correlations are not shown, but are easily computed. The Wilk's values in *Output 6.3* are similar to Likelihood Ratios in Table 5.11 of *UMS*. SPSS assesses these using Chi-SQ rather than F, but conclusions are the same. Eigenvalues are not available in SPSS output.

Standardized and raw canonical coefficients are then printed for each set, producing similar output to that of Table 6.14 in *UMS*. These are useful if scores on canonical variates are to be produced. Loadings for their own and the other set (cross loadings) are then shown. Loadings for variables in their own set correspond to those shown in Table 6.12 of *UMS*. Cross loadings are not shown in Section 6.6.2 of *UMS*. Proportions of variance of each set explained by their own and the opposite canonical variates then follow, corresponding to Table 6.13 of *UMS*. Again, values differ a bit from those produced by SAS, but not enough to change conclusions.

Chapter 7. Multiway Frequency Analysis

This chapter demonstrates hierarchical loglinear analysis using SPSS for Windows for the complete example of Chapter 7, *Using Multivariate Statistics*. The SPSS data set to use is MFA.sav, which can be obtained from the Internet site for this workbook. (See Section 3.1 of Chapter 3 for detailed information on obtaining the SPSS files.)

The example illustrates evaluating relationships among five dichotomous variables about reactions of clinical psychologists who were sexually attracted to their clients. The five variables address issues of whether the therapists thought (1) that their clients were aware of the therapist's attraction to them (AWARE), (2) the attraction was beneficial to the therapy (BENEFIT), (3) the attraction was harmful to the therapy (HARM), as well as whether the therapist had (4) sought consultation when attracted to a client (CONSULT), or (5) felt uncomfortable as a result of the attraction (DISCOMF).

7.1   EVALUATION OF ASSUMPTIONS

The **Crosstabs** command is used to evaluate adequacy of expected frequencies. Each 2 x 2 crosstab table is built individually; hence, you should restrict all tables to cases with complete data. In this example, only values less than 3 are within range. Section 4.1.2 describes how to access the **Select Cases** and the **Select Cases: If** dialog boxes (cf. Figure 4.5). Complete cases are selected by setting up as a condition, AWARE < 3 and BENEFIT < 3 and CONSULT < 3 and HARM < 3 and DISCOMF < 3, as displayed in Figure 7.1. Use these SPSS commands.

```
>Data
    >Select Cases . . .
        ⊙If condition is satisfied
            •AWARE < 3 &
            •BENEFIT < 3 &
            •HARM < 3 &
            •CONSULT < 3 &
            •DISCOMF < 3
    >Unselected Cases Are
        ⊙Deleted
```

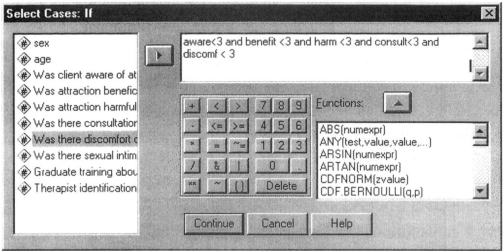

Figure 7.1   **Select Cases: If** dialog box to select complete cases for all analyses.

Return to the main **Select Cases** dialog box and in the **Unselected Cases Are** box, pick the radio button **Deleted**, as shown in Figure 7.2. Now, with all cases having a value of 3 or larger deleted from the data file, only 434 of the original 585 cases remain. (Save this file under a different name if you want to keep the original file intact. Then, use the new file for subsequent analysis.)

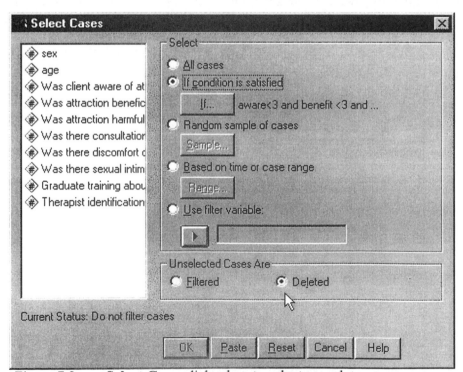

Figure 7.2   **Select Cases** dialog box to select complete cases.

To produce crosstabs for the remaining valid data, follow these SPSS commands.

```
>Analyze
   >Descriptive Statistics
      >Crosstabs
         Row(s):
               •HARM
               •DISCOMF
         Column(s):
               •BENEFIT
               •CONSULT
         >Cells . . .
            Counts
                  ☑Observed
                  ☑Expected
            Percentages
                  ☑Row
                  ☑Column
```

In the **Crosstabs** dialog box, move HARM and DISCOMF into the **Row(s)** listbox, and BENEFIT and CONSULT into the **Column(s)** listbox. Figure 7.3 illustrates this first part of the procedure.

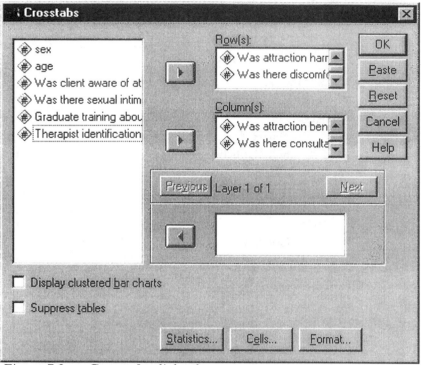

Figure 7.3   **Crosstabs** dialog box.

Follow the remaining SPSS commands for the submenu **Cell Display**, requesting **O**bserved and **Expected** from the **Counts** box and **R**ow and **C**olumn from the **Percentages** box, as illustrated in Figure 7.4.

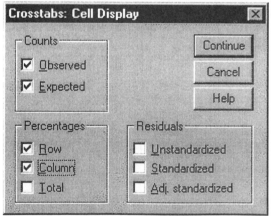

Figure 7.4   **Crosstabs: Cell Display** dialog box.

Navigate back out of the dialog boxes to produce the output in Table 7.14 of *UMS*. Tables for the remaining variables may be produced by repeating this process with appropriate row and column selections.

7.2   HIERARCHICAL LOG-LINEAR ANALYSIS

To produce hierarchical log-linear analysis, follow the SPSS commands below. Figure 7.5 also illustrates the procedure; and, Figure 7.6 shows defining the range for each variable: here "1" is the minimum and "2" is maximum value for all selected variables.

```
>Analyze
    >Loglinear
        >Model Selection...
            Factor(s):
                •AWARE
                    Define Range... (1,2)
                •BENEFIT
                    Define Range... (1,2)
                •HARM
                    Define Range... (1,2)
                •CONSULT
                    Define Range... (1,2)
                •DISCOMF
                    Define Range... (1,2)
            Options . . .
                    ☑ Frequencies
                    ☑ Residuals
                    ☑ Association table
            Delta = 0
```

The choice of **Model Selection ...** is for hierarical analysis.

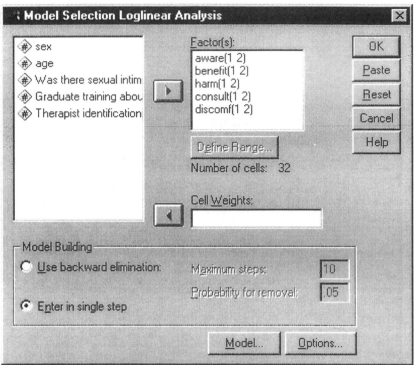

Figure 7.5   **Model Selection Loglinear Analysis dialog** box for model screening.

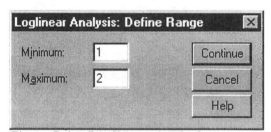

Figure 7.6   **Loglinear Analysis: Define Range** dialog box.

Navigate back out to the main **Loglinear Analysis** dialog box. Note in Figure 7.5 that the **Enter in single step** button is clicked for this initial screening. Continue with the SPSS commands by clicking the **Options...** push button, and making the selections for **Frequencies**, **Residuals** and **Association table**; also, the **Delta** is set to "0". The association table shows the partial associations for all effects, which is useful for screening. The Delta default value is .5 (default for saturated models). Figure 7.7 shows this step.

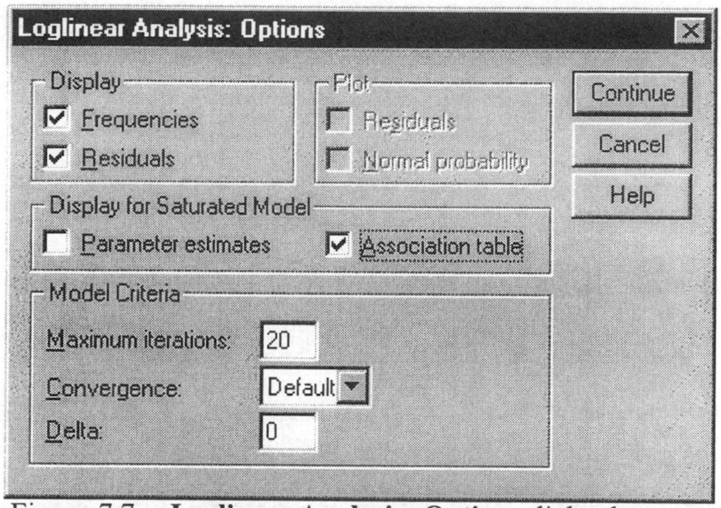

Figure 7.7   **Loglinear Analysis: Options** dialog box.

Back out of the submenu dialog box to the main dialog box and click OK to produce the output, as displayed in Table 7.15 of *UMS*.

To produce the model with all 10 two-way effects with backward elimination, follow these steps: First, in the main **Loglinear Analysis** dialog box, change the **Model Building** from "**Enter in a single step**" to **Use backward elimination** (cf. Figure 7.5). Then, follow these SPSS commands, again starting from within the main **Loglinear** dialog box. This two-way interaction procedure is also illustrated in Figure 7.8.

```
>Model . . .
    ⊙Custom
    Factors = all to Generating Class:
    Build Term(s) = All 2-way
```

To select all the factors in the **Factors:** listbox, highlight them one at a time until all are highlighted (on some computers you may need to also hold the shift key while highlighting factors). Next, from the drop-down list in **Build Term(s)**, select **All 2 way**. Then, click on the right-facing arrow to move all of the factors into the **Generating Class:** listbox.

69

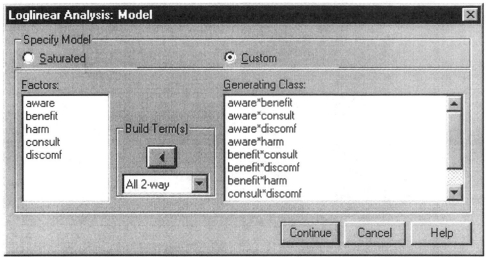

Figure 7.8   **Loglinear Analysis: Model** dialog box for model building.

The output produced is in Table 7.16 of *UMS*. The final table in the output contains observed and expected frequencies, as well as raw and standardized residuals. However, SPSS provides parameter estimates only for saturated (full) hierarchical models.

Residuals are produced by selecting the model with eight (rather than all) of the two-way terms, as seen in Figure 7.9.

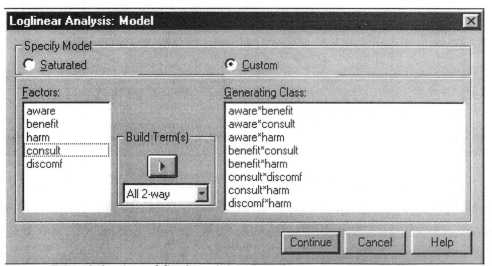

Figure 7.9   Selection of final model with eight two-way associations.

Residuals remain selected as per Figure 7.7. This produces output matching Table 7.17 in *UMS*. The model selection dialog box (which produces hierarchical loglinear analysis) provides parameter estimates only for a saturated model. Further, the most straightforward program for displaying parameter estimates in loglinear analysis, SPSS LOGLINEAR, is unavailable in menus. Therefore, the syntax of Table 7.18 in *UMS* is pasted into a syntax box to produce the corresponding parameter estimates.

Chapter 8. Analysis of Covariance

This chapter demonstrates analysis of covariance using SPSS for Windows for the complete example of Chapter 8, *Using Multivariate Statistics*. The data set to use is ANCOVA.sav on the Internet site. (See Section 3.1 of Chapter 3 for detailed information on obtaining the SPSS files). This example evaluates whether attitudes toward medication are associated with current employment status and/or religious affiliation, after statistically controlling for one's state of physical and mental health and one's use of mood-modifying drugs.

8.1   EVALUATION OF ASSUMPTIONS

Frequencies and histograms are formed as illustrated in Section 4.2.1. of this workbook, noting that the split file procedure must first be used. This provides screening for univariate outliers, sample sizes, normality, and homogeneity of variance. Multivariate outliers are found through multiple regression separately on each group, as discussed in Section 4.2.3. Multicollinearity is assessed through factor analysis as per Section 6.1.

Initial screening procedures reveal the need to apply a logarithmic transform (as demonstrated in Chapter 4) to PHYHEAL, producing LPHYHEAL; and to PSYDRUG, producing LPSYDRUG. (Remember that 1 should be added to PSYDRUG before log transform because it has zeros in the original data.)

Beginning with version 8, SPSS provides for only the General Linear Model (GLM) procedure directly through windows commands. The GLM routines have several desirable features for variance procedures, like ANOVA and MANOVA, including post hoc tests on marginal means (univariate only), Type 1 through Type 4 sums of squares (for handling unbalanced designs), ability to specify multiple random effects models, and saving residuals, predicted values, and influence measures as new variables. (Type I Sums of Square is also available in SPSS MANOVA as "sequential" SS). The MANOVA command can still be accessed but only through syntax. Some advanced MANOVA features are also accessed through the SPSS MANOVA command, such as Roy-Bargman step down tests, dimension reduction analysis, and discriminant coefficients.

Homogeneity of regression is assessed for the covariates of an ANCOVA design through syntax using the MANOVA program. Copy the syntax commands shown in Figure 8.1 into a new syntax file, and click the **Run** button to produce the output. *Output 8.1* shows the results of the analysis.

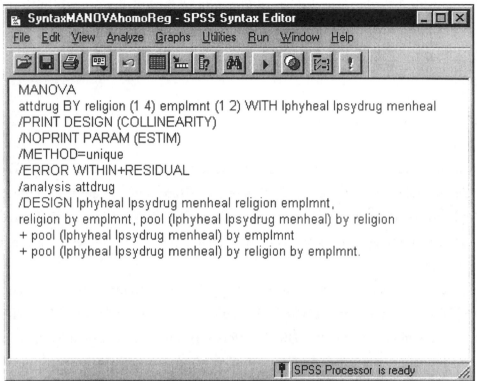

Figure 8.1   Syntax commands for producing test of homogeneity of regression.

Output 8.1   **HOMOGENEITY OF REGRESSION FOR ANALYSIS OF COVARIANCE. PARTIAL OUTPUT.**

```
* * * * * * A n a l y s i s   o f   V a r i a n c e * * * * * *


462 cases accepted.

0 cases rejected because of out-of-range factor values.

3 cases rejected because of missing data.

8 non-empty cells.


1 design will be processed.
```

Tests of Significance for ATTDRUG using UNIQUE sums of squares

Source of Variation	SS	DF	MS	F	Sig of F
WITHIN+RESIDUAL	513.19	430	1.19		
LPHYHEAL	1.18	1	1.18	.99	.320
LPSYDRUG	37.24	1	37.24	31.20	.000
RELIGION	1.87	3	.62	.52	.666
EMPLMNT	.80	1	.80	.67	.412
RELIGION BY EMPLMNT	1.84	3	.61	.51	.673
POOL(LPHYHEAL LPSYDRUG MENHEAL) BY RELIGION + POOL(LPHYHEAL LPSYDRUG MENHEAL) BY EMPLMNT + POOL(LPHYHEAL LPSYDRUG MENHEAL) BY RELIGION BY EMPLMNT	25.98	21	1.24	1.0	.417

The final test is the one that shows homogeneity of regression: the pooled covariates by religion, plus the pooled covariates by employment, plus the pooled covariates by the interaction. Homogeneity of regression is acceptable because Sig of F, at .417, is greater than .05. That is, the hypothesis of homogeneity of regression is not rejected.

8.2 ANALYSIS OF COVARIANCE

The **GLM Univariate** procedure is used for the ANCOVA. Follow these SPSS commands, which are also illustrated in Figure 8.2.

> <u>A</u>nalyze
> >General Linear Model
> >Univariate
> <u>D</u>ependent Variable:
> •attdrug
> <u>F</u>ixed Factor(s):
> •religion
> •emplmnt
> <u>C</u>ovariates:
> •lphyheal
> •menheal
> •lpsydrug

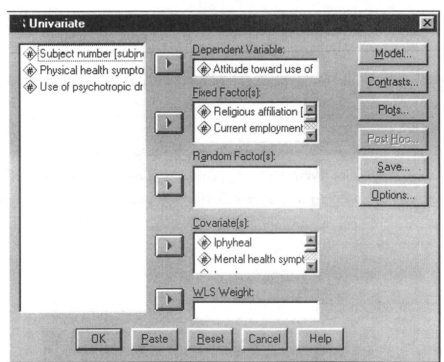

Figure 8.2   **GLM—Univariate** dialog box for ANCOVA.

The **Model...** push button allows you to specify **Type I Sum of squares:**, as shown in Figure 8.3. The default **Full factorial** model is specified.

76

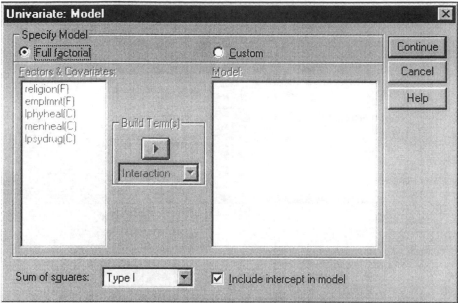

Figure 8.3 **Univariate: Model** dialog box for ANCOVA.

To display observed and adjusted means, use the **Options...** push button of the main **GLM Univariate** dialog box (cf. Figure 8.2) and add the independent variables and interaction to the dialog box, as shown in Figure 8.4. This provides the adjusted (estimated) means. Checking the **Descriptive statistics** box provides the observed (unadjusted) means.

        Options...
            Display Means for:
                •religion
                •emplmnt
                •religion*emplmnt
            Display
                ☑Descriptive statistics

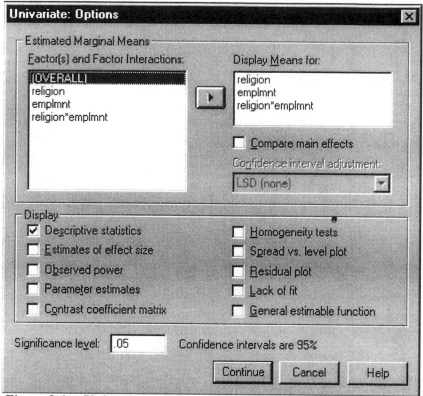

Figure 8.4   **Univariate: Options** dialog box for ANCOVA.

The results are displayed in *Output 8.2*, and match those of Table 8.21 in *UMS*.

Output 8.2   **ANALYSIS OF COVARIANCE OF ATTITUDE TOWARD DRUG USE**

Univariate Analysis of Variance

Between-Subjects Factors

		Value Label	N
Religious affiliation	1	NONE OR OTHER	76
	2	CATHOLIC	119
	3	PROTESTANT	175
	4	JEWISH	92
Current employment status	1	EMPLOYED	245
	2	UNEMPLOYED	217

Descriptive Statistics

Dependent Variable: Attitude toward use of drugs

Religious affiliation	Current	Mean	Std. Deviation	N
NONE OR OTHER	EMPLOYED	7.67	1.35	46
	UNEMPLOYED	7.10	1.18	30
	Total	7.45	1.31	76
CATHOLIC	EMPLOYED	7.67	.98	63
	UNEMPLOYED	8.04	1.09	56
	Total	7.84	1.05	119
PROTESTANT	EMPLOYED	7.51	1.08	92
	UNEMPLOYED	7.84	1.19	83
	Total	7.67	1.15	175
JEWISH	EMPLOYED	7.59	1.11	44
	UNEMPLOYED	7.81	1.21	48
	Total	7.71	1.16	92
Total	EMPLOYED	7.60	1.11	245
	UNEMPLOYED	7.78	1.20	217
	Total	7.68	1.16	462

Tests of Between-Subjects Effects

Dependent Variable: Attitude toward use of drugs

Source	Type I Sum of Squares	df	Mean Square	F	Sig.
Corrected Model	78.683[a]	10	7.868	6.581	.000
Intercept	27278.139	1	27278.139	22817.000	.000
LPHYHEAL	9.908	1	9.908	8.288	.004
MENHEAL	.134	1	.134	.112	.738
LPSYDRUG	45.725	1	45.725	38.247	.000
RELIGION	10.259	3	3.420	2.860	.037
EMPLMNT	3.785	1	3.785	3.166	.076
RELIGION * EMPLMNT	8.871	3	2.957	2.473	.061
Error	539.179	451	1.196		
Total	27896.000	462			
Corrected Total	617.861	461			

a. R Squared = .127 (Adjusted R Squared = .108)

Estimated Marginal Means

1. Religious affiliation

Dependent Variable: Attitude toward use of drugs

Religious affiliation	Mean	Std. Error	95% Confidence Interval	
			Lower Bound	Upper Bound
NONE OR OTHER	7.407[a]	.128	7.155	7.660
CATHOLIC	7.918[a]	.101	7.719	8.116
PROTESTANT	7.660[a]	.083	7.498	7.823
JEWISH	7.644[a]	.115	7.419	7.870

a. Evaluated at covariates appeared in the model: LPHYHEAL = .649596, Mental health symptoms = 6.14, LPSYDRUG = .4159.

2. Current employment status

Dependent Variable: Attitude toward use of drugs

Current employment status	Mean	Std. Error	95% Confidence Interval	
			Lower Bound	Upper Bound
EMPLOYED	7.606[a]	.073	7.463	7.750
UNEMPLOYED	7.709[a]	.079	7.553	7.865

a. Evaluated at covariates appeared in the model: LPHYHEAL = .649596, Mental health symptoms = 6.14, LPSYDRUG = .4159.

3. Religious affiliation * Current employment status

Dependent Variable: Attitude toward use of drugs

Religious affiliation	Current employment status	Mean	Std. Error	95% Confidence Interval	
				Lower Bound	Upper Bound
NONE OR OTHER	EMPLOYED	7.624[a]	.161	7.307	7.942
	UNEMPLOYED	7.191[a]	.201	6.797	7.585
CATHOLIC	EMPLOYED	7.733[a]	.138	7.461	8.005
	UNEMPLOYED	8.103[a]	.147	7.815	8.391
PROTESTANT	EMPLOYED	7.494[a]	.114	7.270	7.718
	UNEMPLOYED	7.827[a]	.120	7.591	8.063
JEWISH	EMPLOYED	7.574[a]	.165	7.249	7.899
	UNEMPLOYED	7.715[a]	.158	7.404	8.027

a. Evaluated at covariates appeared in the model: LPHYHEAL = .649596, Mental health symptoms = 6.14, LPSYDRUG = .4159.

8.3   EVALUATION OF COVARIATES

Obtaining pooled within-cell correlations requires treating the covariates as dependent variables in the **GLM—Multivariate** procedure. Follow the commands below, and as illustrated in Figures 8.5 and 8.6. The residual SSCP, covariance, and correlation matrices are displayed in *Output 8.3*. Note in Figure 8.5 that the **Options** push button is used to activate the **Multivariate Options** dialog box. Then, the **Residual SSCP matrix** check box is selected.

>Analyze
   >General Linear Model
      >GLM – Multivariate...
         Dependent Variable:
            •attdrug
            •lphyeal
            •menheal
            •lpsydrug
         Fixed Factor(s):
            •emplmnt
            •religion
         Options...
            Display = ☑Residual SSCP matrix

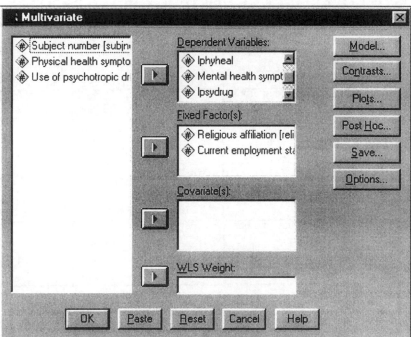

Figure 8.5 **GLM—Multivariate** dialog box for producing pooled within-cell correlations.

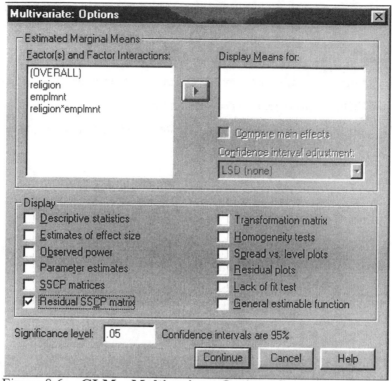

Figure 8.6   **GLM—Multivariate: Options** dialog box for
producing pooled within-cell correlations.

Output 8.3 **SELECTED OUTPUT FOR RESIDUAL MATRICES OF VARIABLES FOR
ANALYSIS OF COVARIANCE OF ATTITUDE TOWARD DRUG USE.**

Residual SSCP Matrix

		Attitude toward use of drugs	LPHYHEAL	Mental health symptoms	LPSYDRUG
Sum-of-Squares and Cross-Products	Attitude toward use of drugs	594.639	12.986	140.173	10.568
	LPHYHEAL	12.986	19.341	201.118	15.634
	Mental health symptoms	140.173	201.118	8054.938	163.469
	LPSYDRUG	10.568	15.634	163.469	12.667
Covariance	Attitude toward use of drugs	1.310	2.860E-02	.309	2.328E-02
	LPHYHEAL	2.860E-02	4.260E-02	.443	3.444E-02
	Mental health symptoms	.309	.443	17.742	.360
	LPSYDRUG	2.328E-02	3.444E-02	.360	2.790E-02
Correlation	Attitude toward use of drugs	1.000	.121	.064	.122
	LPHYHEAL	.121	1.000	.510	.999
	Mental health symptoms	.064	.510	1.000	.512
	LPSYDRUG	.122	.999	.512	1.000

Based on Type III Sum of Squares

Pooled within-cell correlations are in the bottom part of *Output 8.2.*

Chapter 9. Multivariate Analysis of Variance and Covariance

This chapter illustrates procedures in SPSS for conducting a multivariate analysis of variance and multivariate analysis of covariance with the complete example of Chapter 9 of *Using Multivariate Statistics*. To replicate the demonstration, use the file from the Internet site titled MANOVA.sav. (See Section 3.1 of Chapter 3 for detailed information on obtaining the SPSS files.) The examples evaluate several variables as a function of sex role identification, including: high vs. low femininity (FEM) and high vs. low masculinity (MASC). Dependent variables for the multivariate analysis of variance are self esteem (ESTEEM), locus of control (CONTROL), attitudes toward women's role (ATTROLE), socioeconomic level (SEL2), introversion-extroversion (INTEXT), and neuroticism (NEUROTIC).

Three of these variables—SEL2, CONTROL, and ATTROLE—are treated as covariates in the multivariate analysis of covariance. The other three variables remain DVs. Stepdown analysis is not demonstrated in this workbook. SPSS MANOVA is available only through syntax; the SPSS GLM program available through menus does not provide a menu interface for selecting stepdown analysis directly. Rather, it is run through syntax commands. If you want to do stepdown analysis, simply copy the syntax from Sections 9.6.2 and 9.6.3 of *UMS* into the syntax editor and run.

9.1   EVALUATION OF ASSUMPTIONS

Section 4.2 of this workbook demonstrates procedures for obtaining frequency distributions and histograms separately for each group, starting with the **Split File** dialog box. Section 4.2.3 illustrates SPSS commands to identify within-groups multivariate outliers using separate regressions for each group. Box's *M* for homogeneity of variance-covariance matrices is demonstrated in the first full run of Section 9.2.

Homogeneity of regression runs require ANALYSIS and DESIGN paragraphs typed into the syntax editor. First, follow the SPSS commands below to set up the appropriate dialog, shown in Figure 9.1. All six DVs are moved into the **Dependent Variables:** list box. The order of listing DVs follows that of Table 9.14 in the main text: ESTEEM, ATTROLE, NEUROTIC, INTEXT, CONTROL, and SEL2. Of course, FEM and MASC are fixed factors.

The syntax of Table 9.14 in *UMS* evaluates homogeneity of regression for MANCOVA. As a shortcut, you may start the syntax by the following menu choices in GLM and then paste them into the syntax editor. Figure 9.1 shows the Multivariate dialog box choices.

```
>Analyze
    >General Linear Model
        >Multivariate...
            Dependent Variables:
                •esteem
                •attrole
                •neurotic
                •intext
                •control
                •sel2
            Fixed Factor(s)
                •fem
                •masc
```

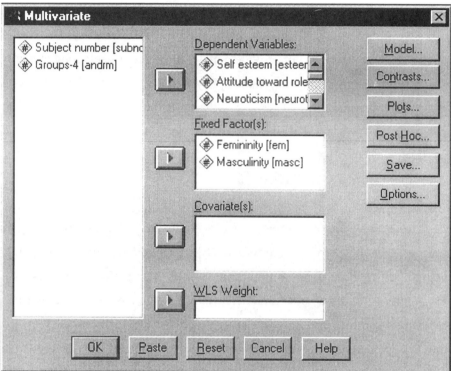

Figure 9.1   **Multivariate** dialog box for MANOVA homogeneity of
regression.

Next, click the **Paste** push button. This causes the syntax box to pop up, with the commands for
choices already made written in. Add to this the syntax as per Table 9.14 of *UMS*, the test of
homogeneity of regression for MANCOVA is produced (also shown in Table 9.14 of *UMS*).

Testing the multivariate assumption for homogeneity of variance is done through the Box's *M* test, described below. Multicollinearity is checked by requesting the determinant of the pooled within-cells correlation matrix in the main MANOVA run of Section 9.2.

9.2   MULTIVARIATE ANALYSIS OF VARIANCE

The Multivariate ANOVA dialog box of Figure 9.1 is used for the main MANOVA run. You will notice immediately within the GLM procedures that there are manifold choices. Only a few are selected here for didactic purposes to match *UMS*; however, you should be aware that interesting choices for analysis abound (cf. Chapter 10 and elsewhere)! Follow these SPSS commands starting from within the main MANOVA dialog box (cf. Figure 9.1), and as shown in Figures 9.2 and 9.3. Notice, too, that not all defaults under the **Model** dialog box are selected, i.e., **Full factorial** is default but **Sums of Squares** is set at **Type I**, sequential. Results are displayed in *Output 9.1*.

>Model
       Sums of squares: Type I
>Options . . .
       Display
              ☑ Descriptive statistics
              ☑ Estimates of effect size
              ☑ SSCP matrices
              ☑ Residual SSCP matrix
              ☑ Homogeneity tests
              ☑ Spread vs. level plots (optional)

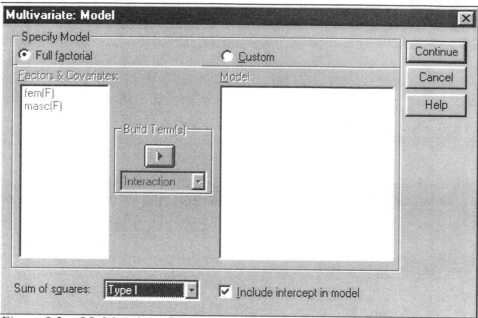

Figure 9.2   **Multivariate: Model** dialog box for main MANOVA run.

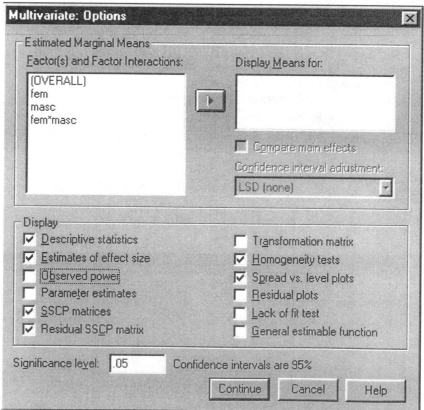

Figure 9.3   **Multivariate: Options** dialog box for main MANOVA run.

General Linear Model

Between-Subjects Factors

		Value Label	N
Femininity	1.00	Low	107
	2.00	High	261
Masculinity	1.00	Low	243
	2.00	High	125

Descriptive Statistics

	Femininity	Masculinity	Mean	Std. Deviation	N
Self esteem	Low	Low	17.9718	3.9132	71
		High	13.8056	3.9411	36
		Total	16.5701	4.3764	107
	High	Low	16.4884	3.4968	172
		High	13.3371	3.0857	89
		Total	15.4138	3.6749	261
	Total	Low	16.9218	3.6779	243
		High	13.4720	3.3447	125
		Total	15.7500	3.9212	368
Attitude toward role of women	Low	Low	34.6761	5.9660	71
		High	29.4722	5.5728	36
		Total	32.9252	6.3137	107
	High	Low	37.0349	6.2957	172
		High	33.3034	6.5356	89
		Total	35.7625	6.6081	261
	Total	Low	36.3457	6.2816	243
		High	32.2000	6.4894	125
		Total	34.9375	6.6418	368
Neuroticism	Low	Low	9.7746	5.1442	71
		High	8.2222	4.8938	36
		Total	9.2523	5.0918	107
	High	Low	8.9826	5.1167	172
		High	7.5393	4.5303	89
		Total	8.4904	4.9634	261
	Total	Low	9.2140	5.1269	243
		High	7.7360	4.6284	125
		Total	8.7120	5.0061	368
Introversion-extroversion	Low	Low	10.2324	3.6964	71
		High	12.2500	3.5986	36
		Total	10.9112	3.7704	107
	High	Low	11.3110	3.6672	172
		High	13.2921	3.3284	89
		Total	11.9866	3.6715	261
	Total	Low	10.9959	3.7008	243
		High	12.9920	3.4266	125
		Total	11.6739	3.7276	368
Locus of control	Low	Low	7.0423	1.3463	71
		High	6.5000	1.1832	36
		Total	6.8598	1.3136	107
	High	Low	6.7733	1.2662	172
		High	6.4607	1.2345	89
		Total	6.6667	1.2619	261
	Total	Low	6.8519	1.2931	243
		High	6.4720	1.2153	125
		Total	6.7228	1.2783	368
Socioeconomic level	Low	Low	38.40765	25.2873969	71
		High	45.31032	28.0048722	36
		Total	40.73004	26.3054271	107
	High	Low	40.27708	24.6760482	172
		High	42.61573	26.1930308	89
		Total	41.07455	25.1777166	261
	Total	Low	39.73086	24.8183865	243
		High	43.39177	26.6413223	125
		Total	40.97438	25.4751541	368

Box's Test of Equality of Covariance Matrices[a]

Box's M	71.180
F	1.083
df1	63
df2	66708
Sig.	.304

Tests the null hypothesis that the observed covariance
matrices of the dependent variables are equal across groups.

a. Design: Intercept+FEM+MASC+FEM * MASC

Bartlett's Test of Sphericity[a]

Likelihood Ratio	.000
Approx. Chi-Square	3775.532
df	20
Sig.	.000

Tests the null hypothesis that the residual covariance
matrix is proportional to an identity matrix.

a. Design: Intercept+FEM+MASC+FEM * MASC

Multivariate Tests[b]

Effect		Value	F	Hypothesis df	Error df	Sig.	Eta Squared
Intercept	Pillai's Trace	.989	5222.298[a]	6.000	359.000	.000	.989
	Wilks' Lambda	.011	5222.298[a]	6.000	359.000	.000	.989
	Hotelling's Trace	87.281	5222.298[a]	6.000	359.000	.000	.989
	Roy's Largest Root	87.281	5222.298[a]	6.000	359.000	.000	.989
FEM	Pillai's Trace	.081	5.274[a]	6.000	359.000	.000	.081
	Wilks' Lambda	.919	5.274[a]	6.000	359.000	.000	.081
	Hotelling's Trace	.088	5.274[a]	6.000	359.000	.000	.081
	Roy's Largest Root	.088	5.274[a]	6.000	359.000	.000	.081
MASC	Pillai's Trace	.244	19.273[a]	6.000	359.000	.000	.244
	Wilks' Lambda	.756	19.273[a]	6.000	359.000	.000	.244
	Hotelling's Trace	.322	19.273[a]	6.000	359.000	.000	.244
	Roy's Largest Root	.322	19.273[a]	6.000	359.000	.000	.244
FEM * MASC	Pillai's Trace	.008	.492[a]	6.000	359.000	.814	.008
	Wilks' Lambda	.992	.492[a]	6.000	359.000	.814	.008
	Hotelling's Trace	.008	.492[a]	6.000	359.000	.814	.008
	Roy's Largest Root	.008	.492[a]	6.000	359.000	.814	.008

a. Exact statistic

b. Design: Intercept+FEM+MASC+FEM * MASC

Levene's Test of Equality of Error Variances[a]

	F	df1	df2	Sig.
Self esteem	1.431	3	364	.233
Attitude toward role of women	.413	3	364	.744
Neuroticism	.767	3	364	.513
Introversion-extroversion	.847	3	364	.469
Locus of control	.408	3	364	.747
Socioeconomic level	.755	3	364	.520

Tests the null hypothesis that the error variance of the dependent variable is equal across groups.

[a] Design: Intercept+FEM+MASC+FEM * MASC

Tests of Between-Subjects Effects

Source	Dependent Variable	Type I Sum of Squares	df	Mean Square	F	Sig.	Eta Squared
Corrected Model	Self esteem	1098.553[a]	3	366.184	29.331	.000	.195
	Attitude toward role of women	2074.441[b]	3	691.480	17.832	.000	.128
	Neuroticism	223.791[c]	3	74.597	3.026	.030	.024
	Introversion-extroversion	415.191[d]	3	138.397	10.755	.000	.081
	Locus of control	15.586[e]	3	5.195	3.237	.022	.026
	Socioeconomic level	1467.970[f]	3	489.323	.752	.521	.006
Intercept	Self esteem	91287.000	1	91287.000	7311.884	.000	.953
	Attitude toward role of women	449191.437	1	449191.437	11583.725	.000	.970
	Neuroticism	27930.533	1	27930.533	1132.949	.000	.757
	Introversion-extroversion	50151.130	1	50151.130	3897.164	.000	.915
	Locus of control	16632.272	1	16632.272	10364.160	.000	.966
	Socioeconomic level	617835.105	1	617835.105	950.078	.000	.723
FEM	Self esteem	101.465	1	101.465	8.127	.005	.022
	Attitude toward role of women	610.889	1	610.889	15.754	.000	.041
	Neuroticism	44.054	1	44.054	1.787	.182	.005
	Introversion-extroversion	87.760	1	87.760	6.820	.009	.018
	Locus of control	2.831	1	2.831	1.764	.185	.005
	Socioeconomic level	9.007	1	9.007	.014	.906	.000
MASC	Self esteem	979.601	1	979.601	78.464	.000	.177
	Attitude toward role of women	1426.757	1	1426.757	36.793	.000	.092
	Neuroticism	179.534	1	179.534	7.282	.007	.020
	Introversion-extroversion	327.408	1	327.408	25.442	.000	.065
	Locus of control	11.859	1	11.859	7.390	.007	.020
	Socioeconomic level	1105.382	1	1105.382	1.700	.193	.005
FEM * MASC	Self esteem	17.487	1	17.487	1.401	.237	.004
	Attitude toward role of women	36.796	1	36.796	.949	.331	.003
	Neuroticism	.202	1	.202	.008	.928	.000
	Introversion-extroversion	2.264E-02	1	2.264E-02	.002	.967	.000
	Locus of control	.895	1	.895	.558	.456	.002
	Socioeconomic level	353.581	1	353.581	.544	.461	.001
Error	Self esteem	4544.447	364	12.485			
	Attitude toward role of women	14115.121	364	38.778			
	Neuroticism	8973.677	364	24.653			
	Introversion-extroversion	4684.179	364	12.869			
	Locus of control	584.143	364	1.605			
	Socioeconomic level	236708.966	364	650.299			
Total	Self esteem	96930.000	368				
	Attitude toward role of women	465381.000	368				
	Neuroticism	37128.000	368				
	Introversion-extroversion	55250.500	368				
	Locus of control	17232.000	368				
	Socioeconomic level	856012.041	368				
Corrected Total	Self esteem	5643.000	367				
	Attitude toward role of women	16189.562	367				
	Neuroticism	9197.467	367				
	Introversion-extroversion	5099.370	367				
	Locus of control	599.728	367				
	Socioeconomic level	238176.937	367				

a. R Squared = .195 (Adjusted R Squared = .188)

b. R Squared = .128 (Adjusted R Squared = .121)

c. R Squared = .024 (Adjusted R Squared = .016)

d. R Squared = .081 (Adjusted R Squared = .074)

e. R Squared = .026 (Adjusted R Squared = .018)

f. R Squared = .006 (Adjusted R Squared = -.002)

Between-Subjects SSCP Matrix

			Self esteem	Attitude toward role of women	Neuroticism	Introversion-extroversion	Locus of control	Socioeconomic level
Hypothesis	Intercept	Self esteem	91287.000	202497.750	50494.500	67662.000	38965.500	237487.50
		Attitude toward role of women	202497.750	449191.437	112009.625	150091.500	86435.375	526807.59
		Neuroticism	50494.500	112009.625	27930.533	37426.565	21553.380	131363.86
		Introversion-extroversion	67662.000	150091.500	37426.565	50151.130	28881.261	176025.93
		Locus of control	38965.500	86435.375	21553.380	28881.261	16632.272	101370.61
		Socioeconomic level	237487.501	526807.592	131363.859	176025.933	101370.6	617835.10
	FEM	Self esteem	101.465	-248.966	66.858	-94.364	16.949	-30.231
		Attitude toward role of women	-248.966	610.889	-164.050	231.542	-41.587	74.177
		Neuroticism	66.858	-164.050	44.054	-62.179	11.168	-19.920
		Introversion-extroversion	-94.364	231.542	-62.179	87.760	-15.762	28.115
		Locus of control	16.949	-41.587	11.168	-15.762	2.831	-5.050
		Socioeconomic level	-30.231	74.177	-19.920	28.115	-5.050	9.007
	MASC	Self esteem	979.601	1182.223	419.371	-566.330	107.784	-1040.593
		Attitude toward role of women	1182.223	1426.757	506.114	-683.470	130.078	-1255.831
		Neuroticism	419.371	506.114	179.534	-242.448	46.143	-445.481
		Introversion-extroversion	-566.330	-683.470	-242.448	327.408	-62.312	601.590
		Locus of control	107.784	130.078	46.143	-62.312	11.859	-114.494
		Socioeconomic level	-1040.593	-1255.831	-445.481	601.590	-114.494	1105.382
	FEM * MASC	Self esteem	17.487	25.366	1.881	-.629	3.957	-78.632
		Attitude toward role of women	25.366	36.796	2.729	-.913	5.740	-114.063
		Neuroticism	1.881	2.729	.202	-.068	.426	-8.459
		Introversion-extroversion	-.629	-.913	-.068	.023	-.142	2.829
		Locus of control	3.957	5.740	.426	-.142	.895	-17.793
		Socioeconomic level	-78.632	-114.063	-8.459	2.829	-17.793	353.581
Error		Self esteem	4544.447	1163.626	2284.390	-758.677	566.811	-1151.359
		Attitude toward role of women	1163.626	14115.121	570.582	90.341	-87.606	944.985
		Neuroticism	2284.390	570.582	8973.677	-59.871	886.883	-691.656
		Introversion-extroversion	-758.677	90.341	-59.871	4684.179	-137.544	1839.977
		Locus of control	566.811	-87.606	886.883	-137.544	584.143	-989.762
		Socioeconomic level	-1151.359	944.985	-691.656	1839.977	-989.762	236708.97

Based on Type I Sum of Squares

92

Residual SSCP Matrix

		Self esteem	Attitude toward role of women	Neuroticism	Introversion-extroversion	Locus of control	Socioecon omic level
Sum-of-Squares and Cross-Products	Self esteem	4544.447	1163.626	2284.390	-758.677	566.811	-1151.359
	Attitude toward role of women	1163.626	14115.121	570.582	90.341	-87.606	944.985
	Neuroticism	2284.390	570.582	8973.677	-59.871	886.883	-691.656
	Introversion-extroversion	-758.677	90.341	-59.871	4684.179	-137.544	1839.977
	Locus of control	566.811	-87.606	886.883	-137.544	584.143	-989.762
	Socioeconomic level	-1151.359	944.985	-691.656	1839.977	-989.762	236708.97
Covariance	Self esteem	12.485	3.197	6.276	-2.084	1.557	-3.163
	Attitude toward role of women	3.197	38.778	1.568	.248	-.241	2.596
	Neuroticism	6.276	1.568	24.653	-.164	2.436	-1.900
	Introversion-extroversion	-2.084	.248	-.164	12.869	-.378	5.055
	Locus of control	1.557	-.241	2.436	-.378	1.605	-2.719
	Socioeconomic level	-3.163	2.596	-1.900	5.055	-2.719	650.299
Correlation	Self esteem	1.000	.145	.358	-.164	.348	-.035
	Attitude toward role of women	.145	1.000	.051	.011	-.031	.016
	Neuroticism	.358	.051	1.000	-.009	.387	-.015
	Introversion-extroversion	-.164	.011	-.009	1.000	-.083	.055
	Locus of control	.348	-.031	.387	-.083	1.000	-.084
	Socioeconomic level	-.035	.016	-.015	.055	-.084	1.000

Based on Type I Sum of Squares

Tests of multivariate effects match those of Table 9.16 in *UMS*. Tests of Between-Subjects Effects correspond to the univariate analyses in Table 9.18 of *UMS*. And, of course, there is no counterpart to the stepdown analysis of Table 9.19 in *UMS*.

9.3   MULTIVARIATE ANALYSIS OF COVARIANCE

The **GLM Multivariate** dialog box (displayed in Figure 9.4) is produced by following the commands given below. The order in which the DVs are entered into the procedure is important for stepdown analysis; however, the order of entering the covariates is not. The choices in the **Multivariate: Model** and **Options** dialog boxes are as per MANOVA (cf. Figures 9.2 and 9.3 respectively). When all options are set up, click on **OK** in the **GLM Multivariate** dialog box to produce *Output 9.2*.

>Analyze
   >General Linear Model
      >Multivariate...
            Dependent Variables:
                  •esteem
                  •intext
                  •neurotic
            Fixed Factor(s)
                  •fem
                  •masc
            Covariates(s)
                  •control
                  •attrole
                  •sel2
    >Model
            Sums of squares: Type I
    >Options . . .
            Display
                  ☑ Descriptive statistics
                  ☑ Estimates of effect size
                  ☑ SSCP matrices
                  ☑ Residual SSCP matrix
                  ☑ Homogeneity tests
                  ☑ Spread vs. level plots (optional)

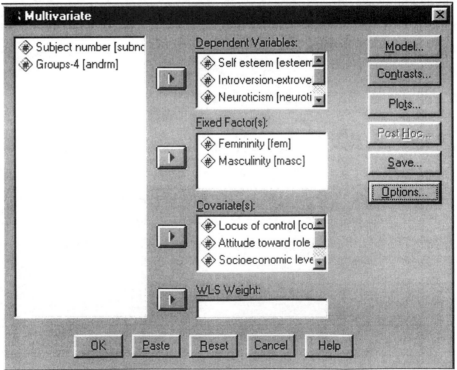

Figure 9.4   **Multivariate** dialog box for MANCOVA.

Output 9.2. MANCOVA OF ESTEEM, INTEXT, AND NEUROTIC WITH ATTROLE, CONTROL, AND SEL2 AS COVARIATES. PARTIAL OUTPUT.

General Linear Model

Between-Subjects Factors

		Value Label	N
Femininity	1.00	Low	107
	2.00	High	261
Masculinity	1.00	Low	243
	2.00	High	125

Descriptive Statistics

	Femininity	Masculinity	Mean	Std. Deviation	N
Self esteem	Low	Low	17.9718	3.9132	71
		High	13.8056	3.9411	36
		Total	16.5701	4.3764	107
	High	Low	16.4884	3.4968	172
		High	13.3371	3.0857	89
		Total	15.4138	3.6749	261
	Total	Low	16.9218	3.6779	243
		High	13.4720	3.3447	125
		Total	15.7500	3.9212	368
Introversion-extroversion	Low	Low	10.2324	3.6964	71
		High	12.2500	3.5986	36
		Total	10.9112	3.7704	107
	High	Low	11.3110	3.6672	172
		High	13.2921	3.3284	89
		Total	11.9866	3.6715	261
	Total	Low	10.9959	3.7008	243
		High	12.9920	3.4266	125
		Total	11.6739	3.7276	368
Neuroticism	Low	Low	9.7746	5.1442	71
		High	8.2222	4.8938	36
		Total	9.2523	5.0918	107
	High	Low	8.9826	5.1167	172
		High	7.5393	4.5303	89
		Total	8.4904	4.9634	261
	Total	Low	9.2140	5.1269	243
		High	7.7360	4.6284	125
		Total	8.7120	5.0061	368

95

Multivariate Tests[b]

Effect		Value	F	Hypothesis df	Error df	Sig.	Eta Squared
Intercept	Pillai's Trace	.976	4803.179[a]	3.000	359.000	.000	.976
	Wilks' Lambda	.024	4803.179[a]	3.000	359.000	.000	.976
	Hotelling's Trace	40.138	4803.179[a]	3.000	359.000	.000	.976
	Roy's Largest Root	40.138	4803.179[a]	3.000	359.000	.000	.976
CONTROL	Pillai's Trace	.248	39.474[a]	3.000	359.000	.000	.248
	Wilks' Lambda	.752	39.474[a]	3.000	359.000	.000	.248
	Hotelling's Trace	.330	39.474[a]	3.000	359.000	.000	.248
	Roy's Largest Root	.330	39.474[a]	3.000	359.000	.000	.248
ATTROLE	Pillai's Trace	.067	8.539[a]	3.000	359.000	.000	.067
	Wilks' Lambda	.933	8.539[a]	3.000	359.000	.000	.067
	Hotelling's Trace	.071	8.539[a]	3.000	359.000	.000	.067
	Roy's Largest Root	.071	8.539[a]	3.000	359.000	.000	.067
SEL2	Pillai's Trace	.005	.570[a]	3.000	359.000	.635	.005
	Wilks' Lambda	.995	.570[a]	3.000	359.000	.635	.005
	Hotelling's Trace	.005	.570[a]	3.000	359.000	.635	.005
	Roy's Largest Root	.005	.570[a]	3.000	359.000	.635	.005
FEM	Pillai's Trace	.046	5.752[a]	3.000	359.000	.001	.046
	Wilks' Lambda	.954	5.752[a]	3.000	359.000	.001	.046
	Hotelling's Trace	.048	5.752[a]	3.000	359.000	.001	.046
	Roy's Largest Root	.048	5.752[a]	3.000	359.000	.001	.046
MASC	Pillai's Trace	.146	20.525[a]	3.000	359.000	.000	.146
	Wilks' Lambda	.854	20.525[a]	3.000	359.000	.000	.146
	Hotelling's Trace	.172	20.525[a]	3.000	359.000	.000	.146
	Roy's Largest Root	.172	20.525[a]	3.000	359.000	.000	.146
FEM * MASC	Pillai's Trace	.003	.316[a]	3.000	359.000	.814	.003
	Wilks' Lambda	.997	.316[a]	3.000	359.000	.814	.003
	Hotelling's Trace	.003	.316[a]	3.000	359.000	.814	.003
	Roy's Largest Root	.003	.316[a]	3.000	359.000	.814	.003

a. Exact statistic

b. Design: Intercept+CONTROL+ATTROLE+SEL2+FEM+MASC+FEM * MASC

Tests of Between-Subjects Effects

Source	Dependent Variable	Type I Sum of Squares	df	Mean Square	F	Sig.	Eta Squared
Corrected Model	Self esteem	1759.395[a]	6	293.233	27.257	.000	.312
	Introversion-extroversion	458.857[b]	6	76.476	5.949	.000	.090
	Neuroticism	1607.951[c]	6	267.992	12.747	.000	.175
Intercept	Self esteem	91287.000	1	91287.000	8485.571	.000	.959
	Introversion-extroversion	50151.130	1	50151.130	3901.413	.000	.915
	Neuroticism	27930.533	1	27930.533	1328.533	.000	.786
CONTROL	Self esteem	806.566	1	806.566	74.974	.000	.172
	Introversion-extroversion	77.623	1	77.623	6.039	.014	.016
	Neuroticism	1487.851	1	1487.851	70.771	.000	.164
ATTROLE	Self esteem	276.191	1	276.191	25.673	.000	.066
	Introversion-extroversion	8.010	1	8.010	.623	.430	.002
	Neuroticism	50.583	1	50.583	2.406	.122	.007
SEL2	Self esteem	3.820	1	3.820	.355	.552	.001
	Introversion-extroversion	17.969	1	17.969	1.398	.238	.004
	Neuroticism	1.674	1	1.674	.080	.778	.000
FEM	Self esteem	134.566	1	134.566	12.509	.000	.033
	Introversion-extroversion	90.520	1	90.520	7.042	.008	.019
	Neuroticism	30.125	1	30.125	1.433	.232	.004
MASC	Self esteem	531.034	1	531.034	49.362	.000	.120
	Introversion-extroversion	264.708	1	264.708	20.592	.000	.054
	Neuroticism	36.192	1	36.192	1.721	.190	.005
FEM * MASC	Self esteem	7.219	1	7.219	.671	.413	.002
	Introversion-extroversion	2.590E-02	1	2.590E-02	.002	.964	.000
	Neuroticism	1.526	1	1.526	.073	.788	.000
Error	Self esteem	3883.605	361	10.758			
	Introversion-extroversion	4640.513	361	12.855			
	Neuroticism	7589.516	361	21.024			
Total	Self esteem	96930.000	368				
	Introversion-extroversion	55250.500	368				
	Neuroticism	37128.000	368				
Corrected Total	Self esteem	5643.000	367				
	Introversion-extroversion	5099.370	367				
	Neuroticism	9197.467	367				

a. R Squared = .312 (Adjusted R Squared = .300)

b. R Squared = .090 (Adjusted R Squared = .075)

c. R Squared = .175 (Adjusted R Squared = .161)

Estimated Marginal Means

1. Femininity

Dependent Variable	Femininity	Mean	Std. Error	95% Confidence Interval	
				Lower Bound	Upper Bound
Self esteem	Low	16.096[a]	.345	15.418	16.774
	High	14.997[a]	.215	14.574	15.419
Introversion-extroversion	Low	11.259[a]	.377	10.518	12.000
	High	12.274[a]	.235	11.812	12.735
Neuroticism	Low	9.064[a]	.482	8.116	10.012
	High	8.410[a]	.300	7.820	9.000

[a.] Evaluated at covariates appeared in the model: Locus of control = 6.7228, Attitude toward role of women = 34.9375, Socioeconomic level = 40.9743791.

2. Masculinity

Dependent Variable	Masculinity	Mean	Std. Error	95% Confidence Interval	
				Lower Bound	Upper Bound
Self esteem	Low	16.965[a]	.234	16.505	17.426
	High	14.127[a]	.341	13.457	14.798
Introversion-extroversion	Low	10.820[a]	.256	10.316	11.324
	High	12.713[a]	.373	11.980	13.445
Neuroticism	Low	9.055[a]	.328	8.411	9.699
	High	8.419[a]	.476	7.482	9.356

[a.] Evaluated at covariates appeared in the model: Locus of control = 6.7228, Attitude toward role of women = 34.9375, Socioeconomic level = 40.9743791.

Note that the SPSS GLM results differ a bit from those of SPSS MANOVA in Table 9.25 of *UMS*, particularly in the multivariate test of FEM. However, there is no substantive difference in the conclusions. Adjusted marginal means are produced using syntax boxes as per Figure 9.5, using the text in Tables 9.29 and 9.30 of *UMS*.

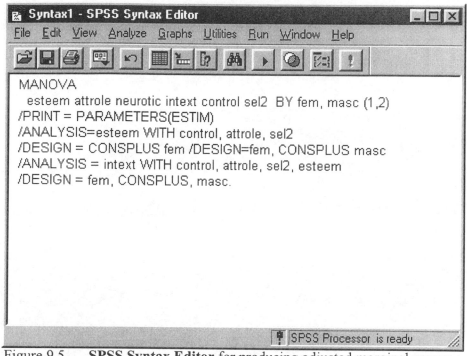

Figure 9.5   **SPSS Syntax Editor** for producing adjusted marginal means.

Chapter 10. Profile Analysis of Repeated Measures

This chapter demonstrates profile analysis of repeated measures using SPSS for Windows for the complete example of Chapter 10 of *Using Multivariate Statistics*. Two data files are used. They are PROFILE.sav and DBMULT.sav. Both files are available on the Internet site. (See Section 3.1 of Chapter 3 for detailed information on obtaining the SPSS files.)

10.1   PROFILE ANALYSIS OF SUBSCALES OF THE WISC

This example assesses variability in subtest scores on the Wechsler Intelligence Scale for Children (WISC) as a function of preference of learning-disabled children for age of playmates (AGEMATE). Levels of AGEMATE are whether children are reported to prefer (1) playmates younger than themselves, (2) playmates older than themselves, or (3) playmates about the same age or no preference. WISC subtests used are information (INFO), comprehension (COMP), arithmetic (ARITH), similarities (SIMIL), vocabulary (VOCAB), digit span (DIGIT), picture completion (PICTCOMP), picture arrangement (PARANG), block design (BLOCK), object assembly (OBJECT), and CODING.

10.1.1 Evaluation of Assumptions

Section 4.2 of this workbook shows how to find frequency distributions and histograms separately for each group, starting with the **Split File** dialog box. As seen in *Output 4.2*, this includes information about missing data as well as distributional assumptions and univariate outliers.

Section 4.2.3 shows how to find within-groups multivariate outliers using separate regressions for each group. Box's *M* for homogeneity of variance-covariance matrices is demonstrated in the run of Section 10.1.2. Multicollinearity is not assessed explicitly, however SPSS GLM prevents variables that cause statistical multicollinearity or singularity from entering the analysis.

10.1.2 Profile Analysis

The following commands produce Figures 10.1, 10.2, and 10.3 for specifying repeated measures multivariate analysis.

>Analyze
    >General Linear Model
        >Repeated Measures...
            Within-Subject Factor Name:
                •subtest
            Number of Levels:
                •11
            Add
       ☑ Define
            Within-Subjects Variables (subtest):
                •info through coding
            Between-Subjects Variables:
                •agemate
       ☑ Options
            Display Means for:
                •agemate
                •subtest
                •agemate*subtest
            ☑ Estimates of effect size
            ☑ Homogeneity tests

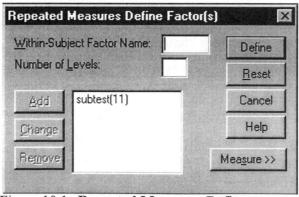

Figure 10.1 **Repeated Measures Define Factor(s)** dialog box.

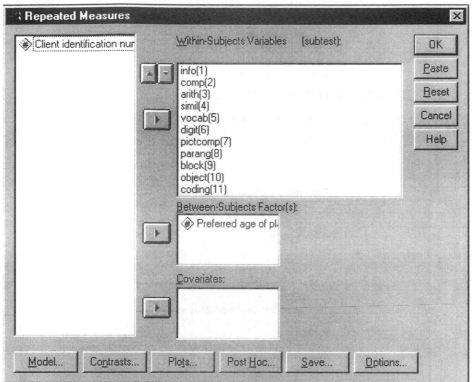

Figure 10.2   **Repeated Measures** dialog box for profile analysis.

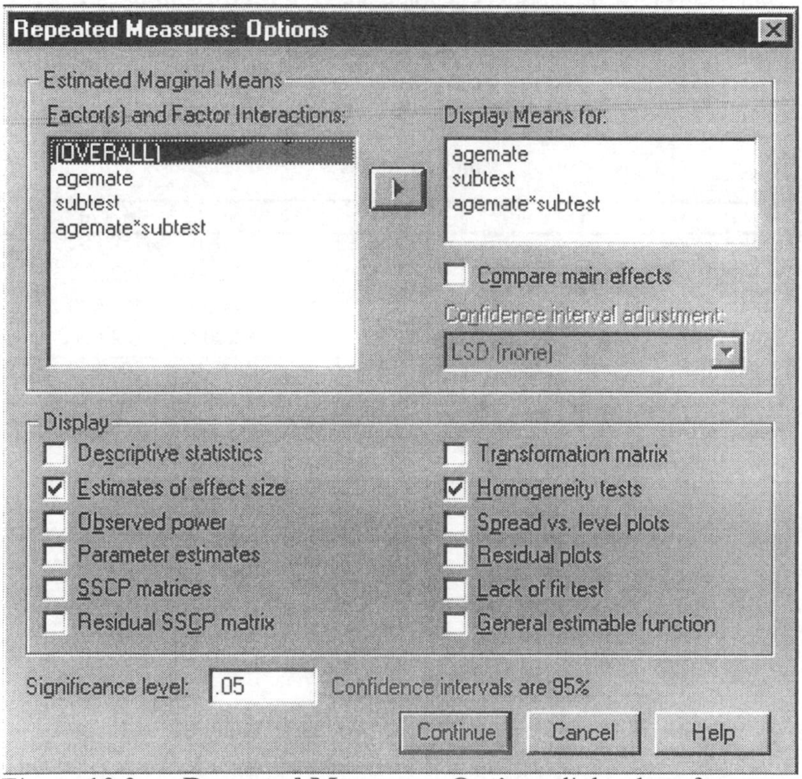

Figure 10.3   **Repeated Measures: Options** dialog box for
profile analysis

103

Clicking on OK produces *Output 10.1*. Results match those of Section 10.6.1.2 of *UMS*. The test for Box's *M* shows no threat to homogeneity of variance-covariances matrices.

Output 10.1. SELECTED OUTPUT FOR PROFILE ANALYSIS OF 11 WISC SUBTESTS

[NOTE: Portions of the output showing univariate approach to repeated measures ANOVA are omitted.]

Between-Subjects Factors

			N
Preferred age of playmates	1		45
	2		54
	3	.	65

Box's Test of Equality of Covariance Matrices[a]

Box's M	126.618
F	.864
df1	132
df2	59321
Sig.	.868

Tests the null hypothesis that the observed covariance matrices of the dependent variables are equal across groups.

a.

Design: Intercept+AGEMATE
Within Subjects Design: SUBTEST

Multivariate Tests[c]

Effect		Value	F	Hypothesis df	Error df	Sig.	Eta Squared
SUBTEST	Pillai's Trace	.464	13.182[a]	10.000	152.000	.000	.464
	Wilks' Lambda	.536	13.182[a]	10.000	152.000	.000	.464
	Hotelling's Trace	.867	13.182[a]	10.000	152.000	.000	.464
	Roy's Largest Root	.867	13.182[a]	10.000	152.000	.000	.464
SUBTEST * AGEMATE	Pillai's Trace	.222	1.915	20.000	306.000	.011	.111
	Wilks' Lambda	.784	1.967[a]	20.000	304.000	.009	.115
	Hotelling's Trace	.267	2.019	20.000	302.000	.007	.118
	Roy's Largest Root	.232	3.551[b]	10.000	153.000	.000	.188

a. Exact statistic

b. The statistic is an upper bound on F that yields a lower bound on the significance level.

c.

Design: Intercept+AGEMATE
Within Subjects Design: SUBTEST

Tests of Between-Subjects Effects

Measure: MEASURE_1
Transformed Variable: Average

Source	Type III Sum of Squares	df	Mean Square	F	Sig.	Eta Squared
Intercept	174789.135	1	174789.135	5724.116	.000	.973
AGEMATE	49.611	2	24.806	.812	.446	.010
Error	4916.227	161	30.536			

Estimated Marginal Means

1. Preferred age of playmates

Measure: MEASURE_1

Preferred age of playmates	Mean	Std. Error	95% Confidence Interval	
			Lower Bound	Upper Bound
1	9.721	.248	9.231	10.212
2	10.146	.227	9.699	10.594
3	9.996	.207	9.588	10.404

2. SUBTEST

Measure: MEASURE_1

SUBTEST	Mean	Std. Error	95% Confidence Interval	
			Lower Bound	Upper Bound
1	9.540	.238	9.069	10.011
2	10.020	.228	9.571	10.470
3	9.052	.196	8.666	9.439
4	10.608	.256	10.102	11.115
5	10.707	.236	10.241	11.173
6	8.763	.206	8.356	9.171
7	10.717	.233	10.257	11.176
8	10.392	.210	9.977	10.807
9	10.329	.217	9.900	10.758
10	10.817	.223	10.376	11.258
11	8.553	.220	8.118	8.988

3. Preferred age of playmates * SUBTEST

Measure: MEASURE_1

Preferred age of playmates	SUBTEST	Mean	Std. Error	95% Confidence Interval	
				Lower Bound	Upper Bound
1	1	9.067	.450	8.178	9.956
	2	9.511	.430	8.663	10.360
	3	9.222	.370	8.492	9.952
	4	9.867	.484	8.911	10.823
	5	10.289	.445	9.410	11.168
	6	8.533	.389	7.764	9.302
	7	11.200	.439	10.333	12.067
	8	10.089	.397	9.305	10.872
	9	10.044	.410	9.234	10.855
	10	10.467	.421	9.635	11.299
	11	8.644	.416	7.823	9.466
2	1	10.185	.411	9.374	10.997
	2	10.426	.392	9.651	11.200
	3	8.796	.337	8.130	9.463
	4	11.204	.442	10.331	12.076
	5	11.463	.406	10.660	12.265
	6	9.019	.355	8.316	9.721
	7	9.796	.401	9.005	10.588
	8	10.704	.362	9.989	11.419
	9	10.296	.375	9.557	11.036
	10	10.907	.385	10.148	11.667
	11	8.815	.380	8.065	9.564
3	1	9.369	.375	8.630	10.109
	2	10.123	.357	9.417	10.829
	3	9.138	.308	8.531	9.746
	4	10.754	.403	9.958	11.549
	5	10.369	.370	9.638	11.101
	6	8.738	.324	8.099	9.378
	7	11.154	.365	10.432	11.875
	8	10.385	.330	9.733	11.036
	9	10.646	.341	9.972	11.320
	10	11.077	.351	10.385	11.769
	11	8.200	.346	7.517	8.883

10.2   DOUBLY MULTIVARIATE ANALYSIS OF REACTION TIME

This example assesses practice effects over four sessions for two target objects: the letter G or a symbol. The two noncommensurate DVs are the (1) slope, and (2) intercept calculated from reactions times over four angles of rotation.

10.2.1   Evaluation of Assumptions

Section 4.2 of this workbook shows how to find frequency distributions and histograms for the eight DVs (four intercept measures and four slope measures) separately for each target type (GROUP). Section 4.2.3 shows how to find within-group multivariate outliers using separate regression for each group. Multicollinearity is not an issue with SPSS GLM because variables causing statistical multicollinearity or singularity are omitted from the analysis. Sample sizes are equal and ratios of variance for all eight variables are well within acceptable limits. Homogeneity of variance-covariance matrices is tested through Box's M in the main analysis of Section 10.2.2

Homogeneity of regression evaluations for stepdown analysis are not run because there is no straightforward way to create within-subjects covariates and run analysis of covariance through SPSS GLM. Therefore, stepdown analysis is impractical. A reasonable alternative, shown here, is to report univariate results along with pooled within cell correlations among original DVs. Another alternative is to use SPSS MANOVA for the analysis, as per Section 10.6.2.2 of *UMS*.

10.2.2   Doubly Multivariate Analysis of Slope and Intercept

For this analysis, use the data set DBLMULT.sav. It is available on the Internet site. (See Section 3.1 of Chapter 3 for detailed information on obtaining the SPSS files.) The following commands produce Figures 10.4 and 10.5 for setting up the doubly multivariate analysis.

```
>Analyze
    >General Linear Model
        >Repeated Measures...
            Within-Subject Factor Name: session
            Number of Levels: 4
            Add
        >Measure>>
            Measure Name:   intercpt
                Add
            Measure Name:   slope
                Add
```

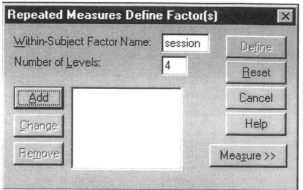

Figure 10.4 **Repeated Measures Define Factor(s)** dialog box for doubly multivariate analysis.

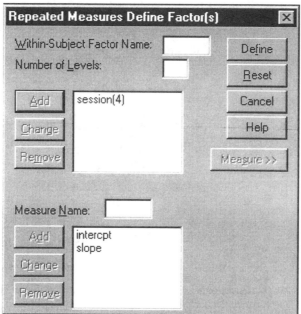

Figure 10.5 Continuation of **Repeated Measures Define Factor(s)** dialog box.

Then, the following commands produce Figures 10.6 and 10.7, which continue the setup for doubly multivariate analysis.

>Define
Within-Subjects Variables (subtest):
  •intrcpt1
  •intrcpt2
  •intrcpt3
  •intrcpt4
  •slope1
  •slope2
  •slope3
  •slope4
Between-Subjects Factor(s):
  •group
☑Options
Display Means for:
  •group
  •session
  •group*session
☑ Estimates of effect size
☑ Homogeneity tests
☑ Residual SSCP matrix

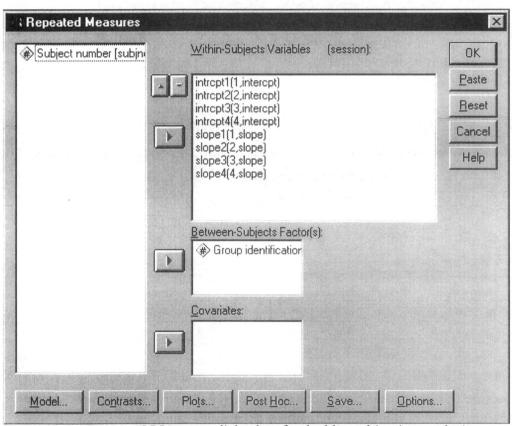

Figure 10.6   **Repeated Measures** dialog box for doubly multivariate analysis.

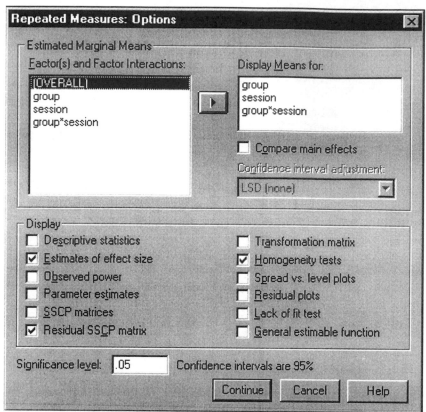

Figure 10.7   **Repeated Measures: Options** dialog box for doubly multivariate analysis.

The request for the residual SSCP matrix produces the pooled within-cell correlation matrix as well. Clicking on the **Continue** pushbutton to return to Figure 10.6; and, then **OK** produces *Output 10.2*, which shows the multivariate omnibus and univariate trend analyses.

Output 10.2 **DOUBLY MULTIVARIATE ANALYSIS OF SLOPE AND INTERCEPT.**

Within-Subjects Factors

Measure	SESSION	Dependent Variable
INTERCPT	1	INTRCPT1
	2	INTRCPT2
	3	INTRCPT3
	4	INTRCPT4
SLOPE	1	SLOPE1
	2	SLOPE2
	3	SLOPE3
	4	SLOPE4

Between-Subjects Factors

		Value Label	N
Group identification	1	Letter G	10
	2	Symbol	10

Box's Test of Equality of Covariance Matrices[a]

Box's M	137.992
F	1.920
df1	36
df2	1090
Sig.	.001

Tests the null hypothesis that the observed covariance
matrices of the dependent variables are equal across groups.

a.

Design: Intercept+GROUP
Within Subjects Design: SESSION

Bartlett's Test of Sphericity[a]

Effect		Likelihood Ratio	Approx. Chi-Square	df	Sig.
Between Subjects		.000	23.079	2	.000
Within Subjects	SESSION	.000	133.023	2	.000

Tests the null hypothesis that the residual covariance matrix is proportional to an identity matrix.

a.

Design: Intercept+GROUP
Within Subjects Design: SESSION

111

Multivariate Tests[b]

Effect			Value	F	Hypothesis df	Error df	Sig.	Eta Squared
Between Subjects	Intercept	Pillai's Trace	.968	255.133[a]	2.000	17.000	.000	.968
		Wilks' Lambda	.032	255.133[a]	2.000	17.000	.000	.968
		Hotelling's Trace	30.016	255.133[a]	2.000	17.000	.000	.968
		Roy's Largest Root	30.016	255.133[a]	2.000	17.000	.000	.968
	GROUP	Pillai's Trace	.730	23.038[a]	2.000	17.000	.000	.730
		Wilks' Lambda	.270	23.038[a]	2.000	17.000	.000	.730
		Hotelling's Trace	2.710	23.038[a]	2.000	17.000	.000	.730
		Roy's Largest Root	2.710	23.038[a]	2.000	17.000	.000	.730
Within Subjects	SESSION	Pillai's Trace	.890	17.453[a]	6.000	13.000	.000	.890
		Wilks' Lambda	.110	17.453[a]	6.000	13.000	.000	.890
		Hotelling's Trace	8.055	17.453[a]	6.000	13.000	.000	.890
		Roy's Largest Root	8.055	17.453[a]	6.000	13.000	.000	.890
	SESSION * GROUP	Pillai's Trace	.821	9.917[a]	6.000	13.000	.000	.821
		Wilks' Lambda	.179	9.917[a]	6.000	13.000	.000	.821
		Hotelling's Trace	4.577	9.917[a]	6.000	13.000	.000	.821
		Roy's Largest Root	4.577	9.917[a]	6.000	13.000	.000	.821

[a]. Exact statistic

[b].

Design: Intercept+GROUP
Within Subjects Design: SESSION

Tests of Within-Subjects Contrasts

Source	Measure	SESSION	Type III Sum of Squares	df	Mean Square	F	Sig.	Eta Squared
SESSION	INTERCPT	Linear	58748.692	1	58748.692	89.445	.000	.832
		Quadratic	5269.587	1	5269.587	19.830	.000	.524
		Cubic	40.840	1	40.840	.340	.567	.019
	SLOPE	Linear	207614.672	1	207614.672	5.517	.030	.235
		Quadratic	755.448	1	755.448	.082	.778	.005
		Cubic	7637.133	1	7637.133	3.902	.064	.178
SESSION * GROUP	INTERCPT	Linear	34539.923	1	34539.923	52.587	.000	.745
		Quadratic	1345.751	1	1345.751	5.064	.037	.220
		Cubic	63.156	1	63.156	.526	.478	.028
	SLOPE	Linear	412.004	1	412.004	.011	.918	.001
		Quadratic	7115.889	1	7115.889	.772	.391	.041
		Cubic	1013.730	1	1013.730	.518	.481	.028
Error(SESSION)	INTERCPT	Linear	11822.707	18	656.817			
		Quadratic	4783.306	18	265.739			
		Cubic	2160.401	18	120.022			
	SLOPE	Linear	677335.981	18	37629.777			
		Quadratic	165948.577	18	9219.365			
		Cubic	35227.344	18	1957.075			

Residual SSCP Matrix

		INTRCPT1	INTRCPT2	INTRCPT3	INTRCPT4	SLOPE1	SLOPE2	SLOPE3	SLOPE4
Sum-of-Squares and Cross-Products	INTRCPT1	38302.080	24205.891	17429.360	13984.292	19292.543	5432.418	4627.504	724.637
	INTRCPT2	24205.891	27756.737	19166.374	15722.735	40187.308	18848.254	5641.159	632.993
	INTRCPT3	17429.360	19166.374	15791.465	13359.841	29481.432	18358.686	2947.886	-372.008
	INTRCPT4	13984.292	15722.735	13359.841	12417.266	40361.631	16309.078	2118.887	-1611.569
	SLOPE1	19292.543	40187.308	29481.432	40361.631	1421244	492087.8	162673.4	96821.145
	SLOPE2	5432.418	18848.254	18358.686	16309.078	492087.8	299824.1	117866.9	92786.629
	SLOPE3	4627.504	5641.159	2947.886	2118.887	162673.4	117866.9	70179.011	62494.468
	SLOPE4	724.637	632.993	-372.008	-1611.569	96821.145	92786.629	62494.468	63255.505
Covariance	INTRCPT1	2127.893	1344.772	968.298	776.905	1071.808	301.801	257.084	40.258
	INTRCPT2	1344.772	1542.041	1064.799	873.485	2232.628	1047.125	313.398	35.166
	INTRCPT3	968.298	1064.799	877.304	742.213	1637.857	1019.927	163.771	-20.667
	INTRCPT4	776.905	873.485	742.213	689.848	2242.313	906.060	117.716	-89.532
	SLOPE1	1071.808	2232.628	1637.857	2242.313	78958.012	27338.212	9037.411	5378.952
	SLOPE2	301.801	1047.125	1019.927	906.060	27338.212	16656.892	6548.163	5154.813
	SLOPE3	257.084	313.398	163.771	117.716	9037.411	6548.163	3898.834	3471.915
	SLOPE4	40.258	35.166	-20.667	-89.532	5378.952	5154.813	3471.915	3514.195
Correlation	INTRCPT1	1.000	.742	.709	.641	.083	.051	.089	.015
	INTRCPT2	.742	1.000	.915	.847	.202	.207	.128	.015
	INTRCPT3	.709	.915	1.000	.954	.197	.267	.089	-.012
	INTRCPT4	.641	.847	.954	1.000	.304	.267	.072	-.058
	SLOPE1	.083	.202	.197	.304	1.000	.754	.515	.323
	SLOPE2	.051	.207	.267	.267	.754	1.000	.813	.674
	SLOPE3	.089	.128	.089	.072	.515	.813	1.000	.938
	SLOPE4	.015	.015	-.012	-.058	.323	.674	.938	1.000

Based on Type III Sum of Squares

Estimated Marginal Means

1. Group identification

Measure	Group identification	Mean	Std. Error	95% Confidence Interval	
				Lower Bound	Upper Bound
INTERCPT	Letter G	124.326	10.240	102.813	145.840
	Symbol	27.641	10.240	6.127	49.154
SLOPE	Letter G	561.502	36.818	484.151	638.853
	Symbol	601.517	36.818	524.166	678.868

2. SESSION

Measure	SESSION	Mean	Std. Error	95% Confidence Interval Lower Bound	95% Confidence Interval Upper Bound
INTERCPT	1	120.776	10.315	99.106	142.447
	2	79.028	8.781	60.580	97.476
	3	56.707	6.623	42.792	70.622
	4	47.423	5.873	35.084	59.762
SLOPE	1	648.560	62.832	516.554	780.566
	2	614.327	28.859	553.697	674.958
	3	542.545	13.962	513.212	571.879
	4	520.605	13.256	492.756	548.454

3. Group identification * SESSION

Measure	Group identification	SESSION	Mean	Std. Error	95% Confidence Interval Lower Bound	95% Confidence Interval Upper Bound
INTERCPT	Letter G	1	200.701	14.587	170.054	231.347
		2	133.754	12.418	107.665	159.843
		3	90.464	9.366	70.786	110.142
		4	72.387	8.306	54.938	89.837
	Symbol	1	40.852	14.587	10.205	71.499
		2	24.302	12.418	-1.787	50.391
		3	22.950	9.366	3.272	42.628
		4	22.458	8.306	5.009	39.908
SLOPE	Letter G	1	642.620	88.858	455.936	829.305
		2	581.127	40.813	495.383	666.872
		3	516.867	19.745	475.384	558.351
		4	505.392	18.746	466.007	544.776
	Symbol	1	654.500	88.858	467.815	841.184
		2	647.527	40.813	561.783	733.272
		3	568.223	19.745	526.740	609.707
		4	535.818	18.746	496.434	575.202

Note that Box's M test suggests significant departure from homogeneity of variance-covariance matrices. However, considering that F < 2, and the notorious sensitivity of the test with almost 1100 df for error, no adjustment for heterogeneity is deemed necessary.

Chapter 11. Discriminant Function Analysis

This chapter demonstrates direct discriminant function analysis with cross-validation and group contrasts using SPSS for Windows, for the complete example of Chapter 11 of *Using Multivariate Statistics*. Use the file DISCRIM.sav on the Internet site. (See Section 3.1 of Chapter 3 for detailed information on obtaining the SPSS files.)

The example demonstrated in this chapter evaluates prediction of work status and one's satisfaction with it (WORKSTAT) by four attitudinal variables, including: attitude towards housework (ATTHOUSE), attitudes toward current marital status (ATTMAR), attitudes toward the role of women (ATTROLE), and locus of control (CONTROL). Groups of women are aggregated by three categories, including (1) currently employed, (2) role-satisfied housewives, or (3) role-dissatisfied housewives.

11.1 EVALUATION OF ASSUMPTIONS

Data screening for grouped data is accomplished in the usual manner, through frequencies and histograms as described in Section 4.2, and using the **Split File...** procedure. Identifying multivariate outliers is accomplished with separate regressions for each group, as described in Section 4.2.3. Deletion of the two cases with extreme values on ATTHOUSE is demonstrated in Section 4.1.2. After deletion, 463 of the original 465 cases remain in the data file.

Homogeneity of variance-covariance matrices are evaluated through Box's *M*, requested in the main discriminant function analysis run of the following section. Multicollinearity is evaluated through a request for the determinant of the pooled within-cells correlation matrix, also in the main run of the following section.

11.2 DIRECT DISCRIMINANT FUNCTION ANALYSIS

11.2.1 Main Analysis

The procedures for evaluating discriminant function analysis begins by clicking on the **Analyze** menu, choosing **Classify**, and then **Discriminant...** . This produces the **Discriminant Analysis** dialog box shown in Figure 11.1. The following commands illustrate the procedure.

>Analyze
>Classify
>Discriminant …
Grouping Variable:
•workstat (1 3)
Independents:
•atthouse
•attmar
•attrole
•control

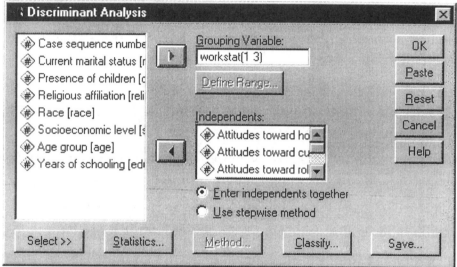

Figure 11.1   **Discriminant Analysis** dialog box.

WORKSTAT is the variable by which groups are separated. It is selected from among the variables list and moved into the **Grouping Variable:** box. Clicking on the **Define Range...** button prompts one to enter the number of levels (beginning and end) of the variable, here it is 1 and 3 as Minimum and Maximum values respectively. ATTHOUSE, ATTMAR, ATTROLE, and CONTROL are selected for the **Independents:** box.

Clicking on the **Statistics...** button in the Discriminant Analysis dialog box produces the **Discriminant Analysis: Statistics** dialog box shown in Figure 11.2. Follow these SPSS commands.

>Statistics…
   Descriptives
      ☑all
   Function Coefficients
      ☑Fisher's
      ☑Unstandardized
   Matrices
      ☑Within-groups correlation

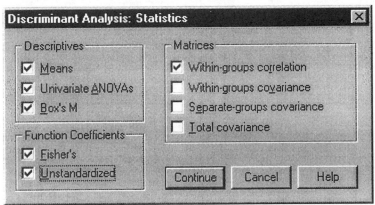

Figure 11.2   **Discriminant Analysis: Statistics** dialog box.

All check boxes within **Descriptives** and **Function Coefficients** are selected, as well as **Within-groups correlation** from the **Matrices** box. Other matrices provide no interesting information here. Clicking on **Continue** returns one to the main **Discriminant Analysis** dialog box. Next, click on the **Classify...** button to produce the next dialog box, called **Discriminant Analysis: Classification**. It is illustrated in Figure 11.3. Follow these SPSS commands.

>Classify. . .
   Prior Probabilities:
      ⊙Compute from group sizes
   Display:
      ☑Summary table
   Plots:
      ☑Separate-groups

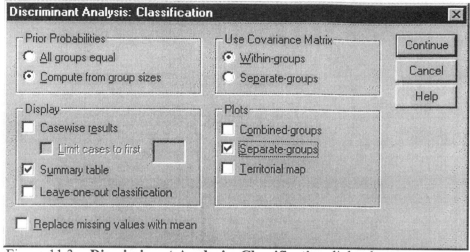

Figure 11.3 **Discriminant Analysis: Classification** dialog box.

From among the options available within **Prior Probabilities**, **Compute from group sizes** is chosen. Choosing **Summary table** from the **Display** box produces the table of classification results. And, **Separate-groups** is selected from among the **Plots** choices, as it displays the most interesting analysis among the choices. Clicking on the **Continue** button again returns one to the **Discriminant Analysis** dialog box. Now, simply, click on the **OK** button to produce *Output 11.1.*

Output 11.1. **DISCRIMINANT FUNCTION ANALYSIS OF FOUR ATTITUDINAL VARIABLES.**

Analysis Case Processing Summary

Unweighted Cases		N	Percent
Valid		456	98.5
Excluded	Missing or out-of-range group codes	0	.0
	At least one missing discriminating variable	7	1.5
	Both missing or out-of-range group codes and at least one missing discriminating variable	0	.0
	Total	7	1.5
Total		463	100.0

Group Statistics

Work Status		Mean	Std. Deviation	Valid N (listwise)	
				Unweighted	Weighted
WORKING	Attitudes toward housework	23.8117	4.4554	239	239.000
	Attitudes toward current marital status	23.3975	8.5300	239	239.000
	Attitudes toward role of women	33.8619	6.9562	239	239.000
	Locus of control	6.7155	1.2378	239	239.000
HAPHOUSE	Attitudes toward housework	22.5074	3.8835	136	136.000
	Attitudes toward current marital status	20.6029	6.6235	136	136.000
	Attitudes toward role of women	37.1912	6.4584	136	136.000
	Locus of control	6.6324	1.3098	136	136.000
UNHOUSE	Attitudes toward housework	24.9259	3.9585	81	81.000
	Attitudes toward current marital status	25.6173	10.2975	81	81.000
	Attitudes toward role of women	35.6667	5.7598	81	81.000
	Locus of control	7.0494	1.2540	81	81.000
Total	Attitudes toward housework	23.6206	4.2786	456	456.000
	Attitudes toward current marital status	22.9583	8.5287	456	456.000
	Attitudes toward role of women	35.1754	6.7590	456	456.000
	Locus of control	6.7500	1.2679	456	456.000

Tests of Equality of Group Means

	Wilks' Lambda	F	df1	df2	Sig.
Attitudes toward housework	.962	8.911	2	453	.000
Attitudes toward current marital status	.959	9.805	2	453	.000
Attitudes toward role of women	.953	11.261	2	453	.000
Locus of control	.987	2.957	2	453	.053

Pooled Within-Groups Matrices

		Attitudes toward housework	Attitudes toward current marital status	Attitudes toward role of women	Locus of control
Correlation	Attitudes toward housework	1.000	.282	-.291	.155
	Attitudes toward current marital status	.282	1.000	-.070	.172
	Attitudes toward role of women	-.291	-.070	1.000	.009
	Locus of control	.155	.172	.009	1.000

Box's Test of Equality of Covariance Matrices

Log Determinants

Work Status	Rank	Log Determinant
WORKING	4	11.379
HAPHOUSE	4	10.317
UNHOUSE	4	11.218
Pooled within-groups	4	11.148

The ranks and natural logarithms of determinants printed are those of the group covariance matrices.

Test Results

Box's M		51.563
F	Approx.	2.537
	df1	20
	df2	245858.2
	Sig.	.000

Tests null hypothesis of equal population covariance matrices.

Summary of Canonical Discriminant Functions

Eigenvalues

Function	Eigenvalue	% of Variance	Cumulative %	Canonical Correlation
1	.077[a]	68.6	68.6	.267
2	.035[a]	31.4	100.0	.184

a. First 2 canonical discriminant functions were used in the analysis.

Wilks' Lambda

Test of Function(s)	Wilks' Lambda	Chi-square	df	Sig.
1 through 2	.897	49.002	8	.000
2	.966	15.614	3	.001

Standardized Canonical Discriminant Function Coefficients

	Function	
	1	2
Attitudes toward housework	.355	.483
Attitudes toward current marital status	.560	.191
Attitudes toward role of women	-.498	.873
Locus of control	.135	.329

Structure Matrix

	Function	
	1	2
Attitudes toward current marital status	.718*	.323
Attitudes toward housework	.679*	.333
Attitudes toward role of women	-.639	.722*
Locus of control	.282	.445*

Pooled within-groups correlations between discriminating variables and standardized canonical discriminant functions
Variables ordered by absolute size of correlation within function.

*. Largest absolute correlation between each variable and any discriminant function

Canonical Discriminant Function Coefficients

	Function	
	1	2
Attitudes toward housework	.084	.115
Attitudes toward current marital status	.067	.023
Attitudes toward role of women	-.075	.132
Locus of control	.107	.261
(Constant)	-1.606	-9.643

Unstandardized coefficients

Functions at Group Centroids

Work Status	Function	
	1	2
WORKING	.141	-.151
HAPHOUSE	-.416	5.393E-02
UNHOUSE	.283	.354

Unstandardized canonical discriminant
functions evaluated at group means

Classification Statistics

Classification Processing Summary

Processed		463
Excluded	Missing or out-of-range group codes	0
	At least one missing discriminating variable	7
Used in Output		456

Prior Probabilities for Groups

Work Status	Prior	Cases Used in Analysis	
		Unweighted	Weighted
WORKING	.524	239	239.000
HAPHOUSE	.298	136	136.000
UNHOUSE	.178	81	81.000
Total	1.000	456	456.000

Classification Function Coefficients

	Work Status		
	WORKING	HAPHOUSE	UNHOUSE
Attitudes toward housework	1.648	1.625	1.718
Attitudes toward current marital status	7.664E-02	4.406E-02	9.771E-02
Attitudes toward role of women	1.081	1.150	1.137
Locus of control	3.223	3.217	3.370
(Constant)	-50.301	-52.009	-56.555

Fisher's linear discriminant functions

Separate-Groups Graphs

Canonical Discriminant Functions

Work Status = WORKING

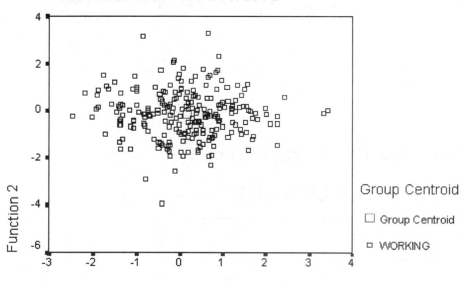

Figure 11.4   Scatterplot of discriminant function scores for
WORKING group.

Canonical Discriminant Functions

Work Status = HAPHOUSE

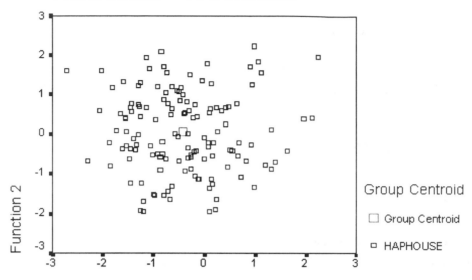

Function 1

Figure 11.5   Scatterplot of discriminant function scores for
HAPHOUSE group.

Canonical Discriminant Functions

Work Status = UNHOUSE

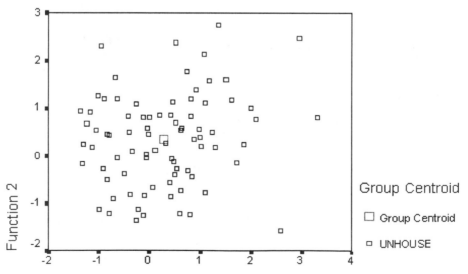

Function 1

Figure 11.6   Scatterplot of discriminant function scores for
UNHOUSE group.

Classification Results[a]

		Work Status	WORKING	HAPHOUSE	UNHOUSE	Total
Original	Count	WORKING	206	31	2	239
		HAPHOUSE	97	37	2	136
		UNHOUSE	66	11	4	81
	%	WORKING	86.2	13.0	.8	100.0
		HAPHOUSE	71.3	27.2	1.5	100.0
		UNHOUSE	81.5	13.6	4.9	100.0

Predicted Group Membership: WORKING, HAPHOUSE, UNHOUSE

a. 54.2% of original grouped cases correctly classified.

Note that Box's *M* indicates possible difficulty with homogeneity of variance-covariance matrices, which can be also evaluated through plots of discriminant function scores. Also, note the discriminant function plots above in Figures 11.4, 11.5, and 11.6.

Note that the scales differ for the three plots, making it a bit more challenging to compare the spread of cases.

11.2.2   Cross-validation of Classification of Cases

Cross-validation of the results is accomplished by randomly selecting 25% of the cases, creating a filtering variable, and then saving selected cases and the filtering variable to a new file. Click on the **Data** menu and choose **Select Cases…** to produce the **Select Cases** dialog box of Figure 11.7, and as shown by the following SPSS commands.

```
>Data
   >Select Cases…
         ⊙ Random sample of cases
               Sample…
```

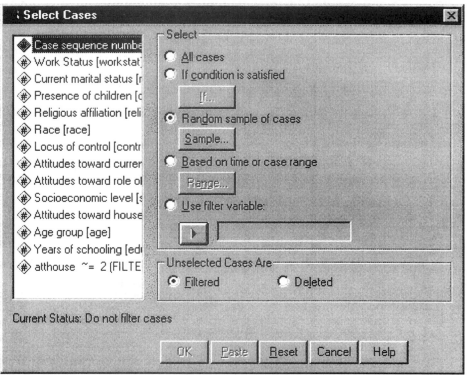

Figure 11.7   **Select Cases** dialog box for random sample of cases.

For the approximate percentage of cases, type in 25, as shown in Figure 11.8. Click on **Continue** to return the **Select Cases** dialog box. Then, **OK** creates the new variable filter_$ in the data file, in which the random sample of 25% cases has a value of 1 and the remaining 75% of the cases have a value of 0. The data file is saved with the new variable, under a new file name. Open this new file to use it for the cross-validation analysis.

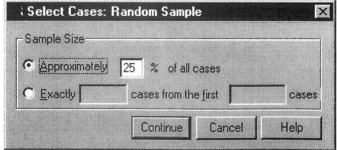

Figure 11.8   **Select Cases: Random Sample** dialog box.

Bringing up the **Discriminant Analysis** dialog box (cf. Section 11.2.1) with the new data file, the **Sel̲ect**>> button is clicked to produce a selection variable box in which to select the SPSS characteristic "filter_$" from the variable list (Figure 11.9).

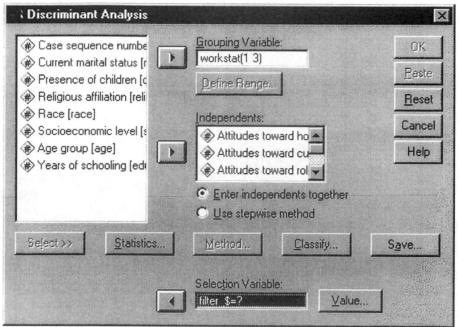

Figure 11.9   **Discriminant Analysis** dialog box with selection variable.

Then, clicking on **V̲alue** brings up the **Discriminant Analysis: Set Value** dialog box, in which the value of 0 (larger set of cases) is typed, as seen in Figure 11.10.

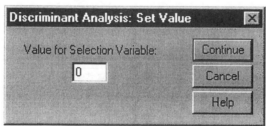

Figure 11.10   **Discriminant Analysis: Set Value** dialog box

Clicking on **Continue** returns the **Discriminant Analysis** dialog box, from which clicking on the **C̲lassify...** button produces the **Discriminant Analysis: Classification** dialog box (cf. Figure 11.3), to choose to **Display** the **Summary Table** and to select **Compute from group sizes** for prior probabilities. Keep covariance matrix to Within Groups. Also, in the **Plots** menu, uncheck (i.e., clear out) the box for separate plots. Then, clicking on **Continue** returns the **Discriminant Analysis** dialog box, where clicking on the **OK** button produces *Output 11.2*. Follow these SPSS commands. Realize, too, that because of the random selection of cases, the output shown here will differ from that in the main text, as well as any other output produced by these procedures.

>Classify. . .
    Prior Probabilities:
        ⊙Compute from group sizes
    Display:
        ☑Summary table
    Use Covariance Matrix:
        ☑Within Groups

Output 11.2. **CROSS-VALIDATION OF CLASSIFICATION OF CASES BY FOUR ATTITUDINAL VARIABLES. PARTIAL OUTPUT.**

Prior Probabilities for Groups

Work Status	Prior	Cases Used in Analysis	
		Unweighted	Weighted
WORKING	.540	195	195.000
HAPHOUSE	.285	103	103.000
UNHOUSE	.175	63	63.000
Total	1.000	361	361.000

Classification Function Coefficients

	Work Status		
	WORKING	HAPHOUSE	UNHOUSE
Attitudes toward housework	1.480	1.470	1.537
Attitudes toward current marital status	.109	7.830E-02	.141
Attitudes toward role of women	1.134	1.212	1.194
Locus of control	3.080	3.143	3.322
(Constant)	-48.802	-51.718	-55.851

Fisher's linear discriminant functions

128

Classification Results[a,b]

			Work Status	Predicted Group Membership			Total
				WORKING	HAPHOUSE	UNHOUSE	
Cases Selected	Original	Count	WORKING	173	20	2	195
			HAPHOUSE	76	25	2	103
			UNHOUSE	49	8	6	63
		%	WORKING	88.7	10.3	1.0	100.0
			HAPHOUSE	73.8	24.3	1.9	100.0
			UNHOUSE	77.8	12.7	9.5	100.0
Cases Not Selected	Original	Count	WORKING	38	7	1	46
			HAPHOUSE	27	5	1	33
			UNHOUSE	15	3	0	18
		%	WORKING	82.6	15.2	2.2	100.0
			HAPHOUSE	81.8	15.2	3.0	100.0
			UNHOUSE	83.3	16.7	.0	100.0

a. 56.5% of selected original grouped cases correctly classified.

b. 44.3% of unselected original grouped cases correctly classified.

Note that the results of cross-validation classification differ from what is shown in *Using Multivariate Statistics* because a different random sample of cases was used for the analysis.

Chapter 12. Logistic Regression

This chapter demonstrates SPSS for Windows procedures for logistic regression for the complete examples of Chapter 12, *Using Multivariate Statistics*. The file to use is LOGREG.sav. (See Section 3.1 of Chapter 3 for detailed information on obtaining the SPSS files.) The first example evaluates prediction of two levels of work status: whether a woman is employed outside the home for more than 20 hours per week. Predictor variables are attitude toward housework (ATTHOUSE), attitude toward current marital status (ATTMAR), attitude toward role of women (ATTROLE) and locus of control (CONTROL). The second example predicts three levels of work status: working women (employed outside the home more than 20 hours per week), role-satisfied housewives, and role-dissatisfied housewives and adds several demographic variables: current MARITAL status, RELIGION (religious affiliation), SEL (socioeconomic level), presence of CHILDREN, RACE, AGE, and EDUCational level attained. The analysis is sequential, first entering demographic variables, and then evaluating whether attitudinal variables enhance prediction over that afforded by demographic variables.

12.1 EVALUATION OF ASSUMPTIONS

Values of zero on SEL are declared missing as per Section 3.2. Commands to evaluate and replace missing data are:

>Analyze
>Missing Value Analysis...
Quantitative Variables:
- control
- attmar
- attrole
- sel
- atthouse
- age
- educ
Categorical Variables:
- workstat
- marital
- children
- religion
- race
☑EM
>Descriptives...
☑t-tests with groups formed by indicator variables

131

☑Include probabilities in table
☑Crosstabulations of categorical and indicator variables
Omit variables missing less than __1__ % of cases
>Patterns...
☑Cases with missing values, sorted by missing value patterns
Variables
Additional information for:
all except RACE
>EM...
☑Save completed data
>File...
LOGREGC.SAV

Figure 12.1 shows the main dialog box for **Missing Value Analysis**, in which the selected **Quantitative** and **Categorical variables** are selected, along with **EM** to designate the type of estimation of missing values.

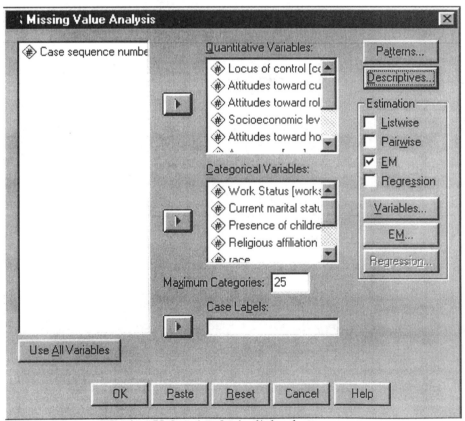

Figure 12.1   **Missing Value Analysis** dialog box.

Selecting **Descriptives** produces the **Missing Value Analysis: Descriptives** dialog box (cf. Fiigure 12.2) to choose the desired descriptive statistics and change the criterion for omission of variables missing from 5% to 1% of the cases.

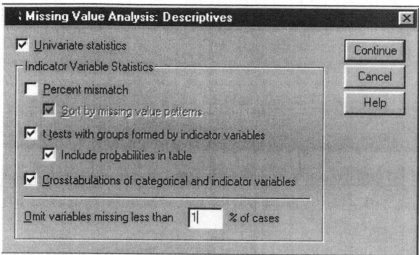

Figure 12.2   **Missing Value Analysis: Descriptives** dialog box.

Clicking on **Continue** returns the **Missing Value Analysis** dialog box of Figure 12.1, in which **Patterns...** is selected, producing the **Missing Value Analysis: Patterns** dialog box of Figure 12.3.

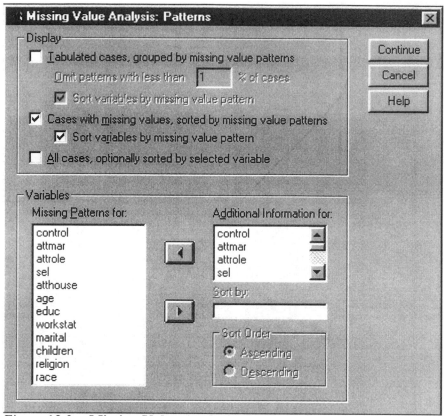

Figure 12.3   **Missing Value Analysis: Patterns** dialog box.

The pattern chosen is **Cases with missing values**, and **Additional Information for** all variables except RACE is requested. Clicking on **Continue** again returns the main dialog box of Figure 12.1, in which the **EM...** radio button is clicked. This produces the **Missing Value Analysis: EM** dialog box of Figure 12.4.

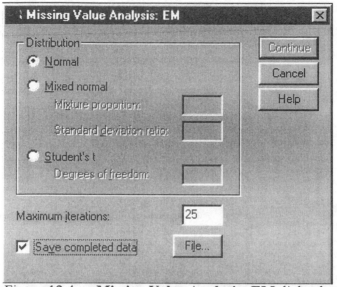

Figure 12.4   **Missing Value Analysis: EM** dialog box.

Default values are retained, and the request is made to **Save completed data**. The **File...** radio button is then clicked, which produces the usual **Save Data As** dialog box, in which the file to be saved is named LOGREGC.

Clicking on **Continue** and then **OK** then produces the output shown in Table 12.12 of *UMS*, and creates the LOGREGC.SAV with imputed values. Cases with missing values on RELIGION are omitted from further analysis using the procedures of Section 4.1.2 (cases are selected on the basis of religion > 0).

Adequacy of expected frequencies is evaluated as per the **Crosstabs** dialog boxes of Figures 7.3 and 7.4 in Section 7.1 this workbook.. Two runs are required, substituting the variables indicated in Table 12.13 of *UMS*. (You may optionally limit the cell display to **Observed and Expected Counts**, and omit **Percentages**.) This produces the output of Table 12.13 of *UMS*. Linearity in the logit is tested as part of the following analyses.

12.2   DIRECT LOGISTIC REGRESSION WITH TWO-CATEGORY OUTCOME

Cases with missing values on RELIGION must be omitted from the analysis, to make it consistent with the sequential three-outcome analysis of Section 12.3. This is done by selecting cases with values of RELIGION > 0, which eliminates cases with system-missing (.) values on religion from the direct logistic regression analysis.

WORKSTAT must be recoded to combine the two housewife groups, by choosing the **Transform** menu, clicking on the **Recode** submenu, and then clicking on **Into Same Variables...** which produces the **Recode into Same Variables** dialog box, as shown in Figure 12.5. Follow these SPSS commands, as shown in Figure 12.5 and 12.6. (Note, save the data set with recoded values of WORKSTAT under a new file name, such as LOGREGX.SAV, so that the original file may be retrieved for the analysis of Section 12.3.)

>Transform
    >Recode
        >Into Same Variables...

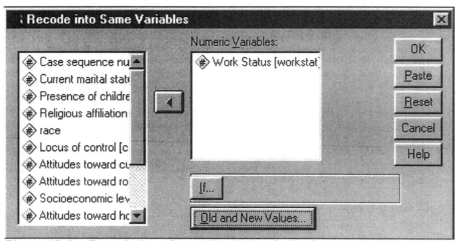

Figure 12.5   **Recode into Same Variables** dialog box.

After adding WORKSTAT, clicking on the **Old and New Values...** button produces the **Recode into Same Variables: Old and New Values** dialog box of Figure 12.6.

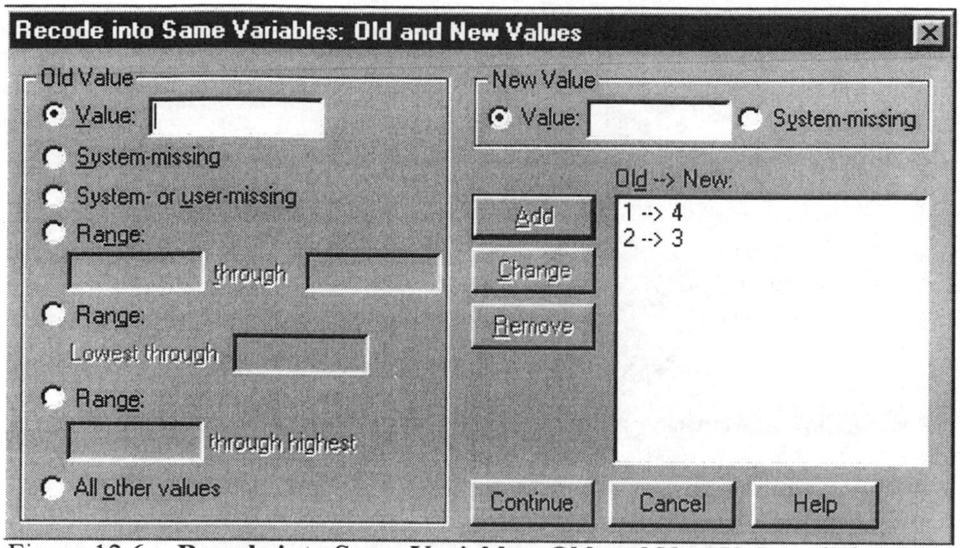

Figure 12.6 **Recode into Same Variables: Old and New Values** dialog box.

Note that group 1 (WORKING women) should be recoded as 4, and group 2 recoded to 3 (to combine it with group 3). This recode produces output consistent with Table 12.14 in *Using Multivariate Statistics*, with the first group as the "response" category. (SPSS considers the group with the highest indicator code to be the response group.) To recode group 1 into group 4, type 1 in the **Old Value** box, 4 in the **New Value** box, and then click on the **Add** button next to the **Old --> New:** box. Then type 2 in the **Old Value** box, 3 in the **New Value** box, and click on the **Add** button again to combine group 2 with group 3. Clicking on the **Continue** button returns the **Recode into Same Variables** dialog box, where clicking on the **OK** button modifies the data file. Value labels also need to be changed, so that 4=WORKING and 3 = HOUSEWFE.

Interactions to test linearity of the logit are created using the following for each of the four continuous variables: control, attmar, attrole, atthouse (only the transformation for control is shown in Figure 12.7).

```
>Transform
    >Compute...
        Target Variable: lin_ctrl
        Numeric Expression: control*LN(control)
```

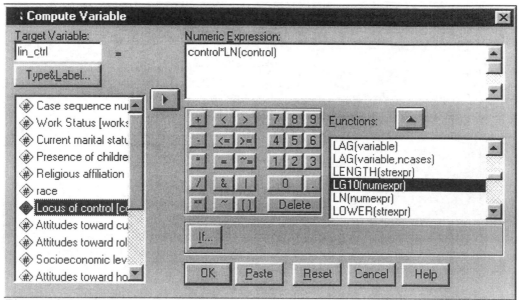

Figure 12.7 **Compute Variable** dialog box with Target Variable and Numeric Expression shown.

After creating interactions for the remaining three variables, a two-category direct logistic regression analysis is performed which uses the four original continuous variables and four interactions as predictors, using the new data set with recoded values of WORKSTAT. This is done through the **Regression** submenu of **Analyze**, and then **Binary Logistic** regression. Then, enter the dependent variable and covariates, as shown in Figure 12.8. Follow these SPSS commands. Optionally, one may elect to produce the chart of predicted probabilities.

>Analyze
    >Regression
        >Binary Logistic
            Dependent:
                · workstat
            Covariates:
                •atthouse
                •attmar
                •attrole
                •control
                •lin_aths
                •lin_atmr
                •lin_atrl
                •lin_ctrl

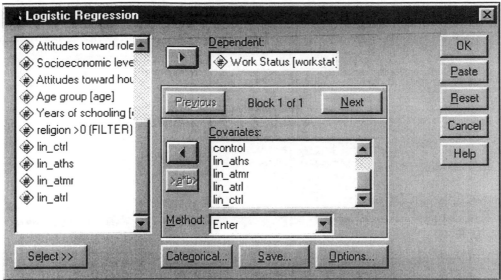

Figure 12.8   Binary **Logistic Regression** dialog box to test linearity in the logit.

Clicking on **OK** produces *Output 12.1.*

Output 12.1   **SYNTAX AND SELECTED OUTPUT OF SPSS BINARY LOGISTIC REGRESSION TO TEST LINEARITY IN THE LOGIT.**

Variables in the Equation

		B	S.E.	Wald	df	Sig.	Exp(B)
Step 1[a]	ATTHOUSE	-.814	.629	1.674	1	.196	.443
	ATTMAR	.222	.234	.895	1	.344	1.248
	ATTROLE	-1.556	.623	6.240	1	.012	.211
	CONTROL	1.970	2.177	.819	1	.366	7.171
	LIN_ATHS	.189	.152	1.543	1	.214	1.208
	LIN_ATMR	-.048	.055	.750	1	.386	.954
	LIN_ATRL	.326	.136	5.742	1	.017	1.386
	LIN_CTRL	-.686	.740	.861	1	.354	.504
	Constant	12.846	7.399	3.014	1	.083	379249.5

[a.] Variable(s) entered on step 1: ATTHOUSE, ATTMAR, ATTROLE, CONTROL, LIN_ATHS, LIN_ATMR, LIN_ATRL, LIN_CTRL.

The main two-category direct analysis is accomplished as per Figure 12.8, omitting the interactions, as seen in Figure 12.9. Optionally, one may elect to produce the chart of predicted probabilities.

139

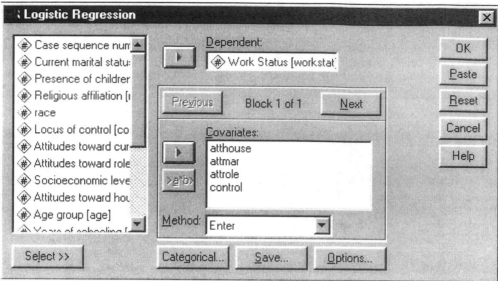

Figure 12.9   Binary **Logistic Regression** dialog box.

A classification plot is produced by clicking on the **Options** button, and choosing **Classification plots**, as per Figure 12.10. Results are in *Output 12.2.*

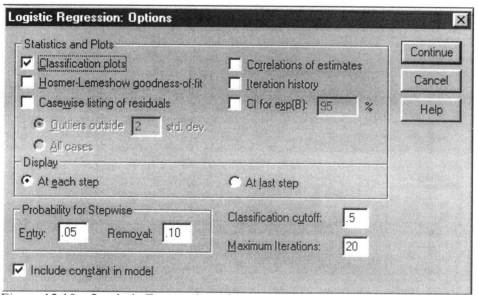

Figure 12.10   **Logistic Regression: Options** dialog box to select classification plots.

Output 12.2. **LOGISTIC REGRESSION OF WORK STATUS WITH FOUR ATTITUDINAL VARIABLES. SELECTED OUTPUT.**

Logistic Regression

Case Processing Summary

Unweighted Cases [a]		N	Percent
Selected Cases	Included in Analysis	462	100.0
	Missing Cases	0	.0
	Total	462	100.0
Unselected Cases		0	.0
Total		462	100.0

a. If weight is in effect, see classification table for the total
number of cases.

Dependent Variable Encoding

Original Value	Internal Value
Role-dissatisfied housewives	0
4.00	1

Block 0: Beginning Block

Classification Table[a,b]

			Predicted		
			Work Status		
			Role-dissati sfied housewives	4.00	Percentage Correct
Observed					
Step 0	Work Status	Role-dissatisfied housewives	0	217	.0
		4.00	0	245	100.0
	Overall Percentage				53.0

a. Constant is included in the model.

b. The cut value is .500

Variables in the Equation

		B	S.E.	Wald	df	Sig.	Exp(B)
Step 0	Constant	.121	.093	1.695	1	.193	1.129

Variables not in the Equation

			Score	df	Sig.
Step 0	Variables	ATTHOUSE	.184	1	.668
		ATTMAR	1.727	1	.189
		ATTROLE	19.768	1	.000
		CONTROL	.533	1	.465
	Overall Statistics		22.747	4	.000

Block 1: Method = Enter

Omnibus Tests of Model Coefficients

		Chi-square	df	Sig.
Step 1	Step	23.244	4	.000
	Block	23.244	4	.000
	Model	23.244	4	.000

Model Summary

Step	-2 Log likelihood	Cox & Snell R Square	Nagelkerke R Square
1	615.526	.049	.066

Classification Table[a]

			Predicted		
			Work Status		
			Role-dissatisfied housewives	4.00	Percentage Correct
	Observed				
Step 1	Work Status	Role-dissatisfied housewives	107	110	49.3
		4.00	79	166	67.8
	Overall Percentage				59.1

a. The cut value is .500

Variables in the Equation

		B	S.E.	Wald	df	Sig.	Exp(B)
Step 1[a]	ATTHOUSE	-.028	.024	1.401	1	.237	.972
	ATTMAR	.016	.012	1.826	1	.177	1.016
	ATTROLE	-.068	.015	19.292	1	.000	.934
	CONTROL	-.057	.078	.542	1	.462	.944
	Constant	3.196	.958	11.128	1	.001	24.431

a. Variable(s) entered on step 1: ATTHOUSE, ATTMAR, ATTROLE, CONTROL.

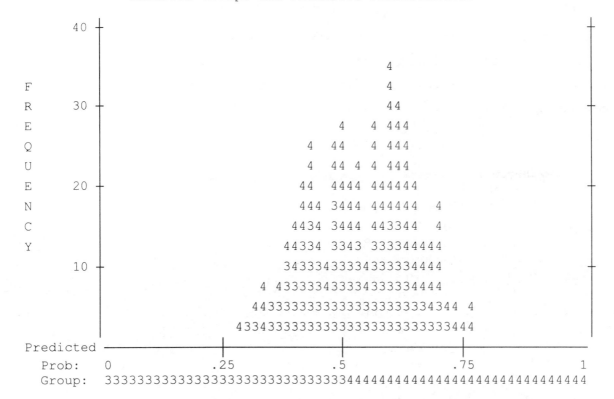

```
          Step number: 1

          Observed Groups and Predicted Probabilities

     40 +                                                            +
   F
   R     30 +                            4                           +
   E                                     4
   Q                                    44
   U                           4     4 444
   E                     4  44    4 444
   N                     4  44 4 4 444
   C     20 +          44   4444 444444                              +
   Y                   444 3444 444444   4
              4434 3444 443344   4
              44334 3343 333344444
     10 +     34333433334333334444                                   +
            4 433333433334333334444
            44333333333333333333334344  4
            433433333333333333333333333444
   Predicted ─────────┼───────────┼───────────┼───────────────────
       Prob:  0        .25         .5          .75          1
      Group:  33333333333333333333333333333333344444444444444444444444444444444444
```

Predicted Probability is of Membership for 4.00
The Cut Value is .50
Symbols: 3 - Role-dissatisfied housewives
         4 - 4.00
Each Symbol Represents 2.5 Cases.

Model Chi-Square and B values match the model test and parameter estimates of Table 12.14 in *UMS*. However, the classification results for SPSS are quite different from those of Table 12.14 because prediction success rather than classification is requested in the *UMS* run. SPSS provides Cox & Snell and Nagelkerke measures of strength of association (cf. Section 12.6.3 of *UMS*).

The model that excludes ATTROLE is produced by eliminating it from the list of covariates in Figure 12.7. Output corresponds to that of Table 12.15 in *UMS*.

12.3 SEQUENTIAL LOGISTIC REGRESSION WITH THREE CATEGORIES OF OUTCOME

First, it is necessary to retrieve the file (LOGREGC.SAV) in which WORKSTAT has its original three-category codes. Then, the following commands produce Figure 12.11 for testing linearity in the logit, in which all variables plus interactions are included. (Interactions for demographic variables are produced as per Figure 12.7.)

```
>Analyze
   >Regression
      >Multinomial Logistic...
         Dependent:
            •workstat
         Factor(s):
            •marital
            •children
            •religion
            •race
         Covariate(s):
            •control
            •attmar
            •attrole
            •atthouse
            •sel
            •age
            •educ
            •lin_cntr
            •lin_atmr
            •lin_atrl
            •lin_aths
            •lin_sel
            •lin_age
            •lin_educ
```

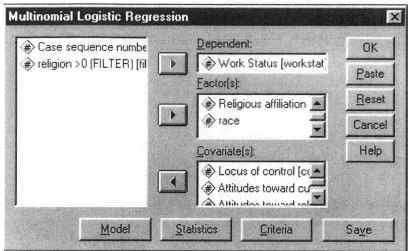

Figure 12.11   **Multinomial Logistic Regression** dialog box to test
                for linearity in the logit.

Table 12.19 in *UMS* shows the results of the test.

The main analysis is produced by the following commands, which produce Figures 12.12 and

12.13:

```
>Analyze
  >Regression
    >Multinomial Logistic...
        Dependent:
            •workstat
        Factor(s):
            •marital
            •children
            •religion
            •race
        Covariate(s):
            •control
            •attmar
            •attrole
            •atthouse
            •sel
            •age
            •educ
        >Statistics
            ☑Classification table
            ☑Goodness of fit chi-square statistics
```

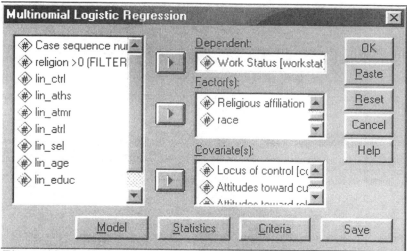

Figure 12.12 **Multinomial Logistic Regression** dialog box.

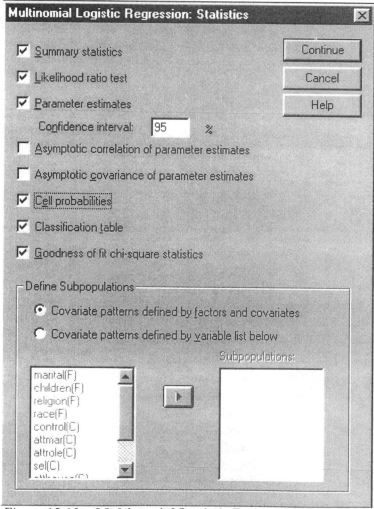

Figure 12.13 **Multinomial Logistic Regression: Statistics**
dialog box.

Note that the first three boxes in Figure 12.13 are checked by default. Clicking on **Continue** and then **OK** produces the output of Table 12.20 in UMS. The output of Table 12.21 in UMS is produced by omitting the attitudinal variables (CONTROL, ATTMAR, ATTROLE, and ATTHOUSE) from the list of Covariates in Figure 12.11.

Chapter 13. Principal Components and Factor Analysis

This chapter demonstrates factor analysis using SPSS for Windows for the complete example of Chapter 13 of Using Multivariate Statistics. The file to use is WFACTOR.sav on the Internet site. (See Section 3.1 of Chapter 3 for detailed information on obtaining the SPSS files.) This example demonstrates factor analysis of the Bem Sex Role Inventory.

13.1   EVALUATION OF ASSUMPTIONS

Distributions of the 44 variables are examined for skewness through the Frequencies command (cf. Section 4.1.1). And, spot checks for linearity are conducted by examining scatterplots, as demonstrated in Section 4.1.4.

The most convenient way in SPSS to identify outliers (when it is suspected that there are many—the procedures of Section 4.1.7 are inconvenient if there are many outliers) is through logistic or linear regression. Other procedures appropriate to this circumstance are not plainly available in SPSS: Discriminant function analysis provides no significance tests for variables adjusted for each other and MANOVA would require separate runs for each variable, inconvenient when there are many variables. Outliers among cases may be found through regression using SUBNO as the dummy DV, as described in Section 4.1.6. Save the new variable mah_1, the Mahalanobis distance for each case. For the data in the current file, WFACTOR.sav, logistic regression was unable to find a unique solution; hence, stepwise linear regression was chosen.

It is first necessary to create the dummy variable for regression. To do this, follow these SPSS commands to create a dummy variable with a code of zero for all cases, as demonstrated in Figure 4.15, and in the following commands.

```
>Transform
    >Compute . . .
        Target Variable: = dummy
        Numeric Expression: = 0
```

Then, instead of changing the file itself, the value for DUMMY is changed for each case in which the Mahalanobis distance is greater than 78.75, the critical value at $\alpha = .001$ for 44 variables. Now, follow these SPSS commands to access the **Recode into Same Variables** dialog box of Figures 13.1. and 13.2.

>Transform
   >Recode
      Into Same Variables . . .
         Numeric Variables: dummy
         If...
         ⊙Include if case satisfies condition: mah_1 > 78.75

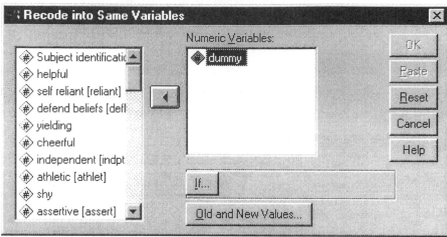

Figure 13.1   **Recode into Same Variables** dialog box to recode
DUMMY for outliers.

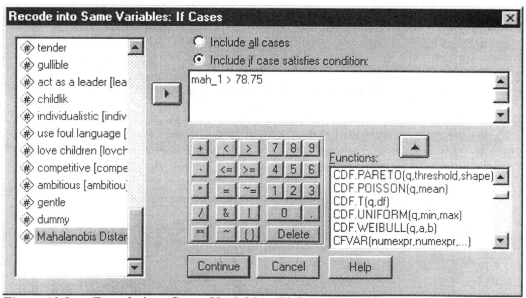

Figure 13.2   **Recode into Same Variables: If Cases** dialog box to recode
DUMMY for outliers.

Click Continue to return to the **Recode into Same Variables** dialog box and select the Old and New Values button. Now, progress in the procedure by typing in 0 for Old Value and 1 for the New Value, then **Add**. Follow these commands, and as shown in Figure 13.3

```
>Old and New Values...
      >Old Value
            ⊙Value  =  0
      >New Value
            ⊙Value  =  1
                  Old –> New
                        Add
```

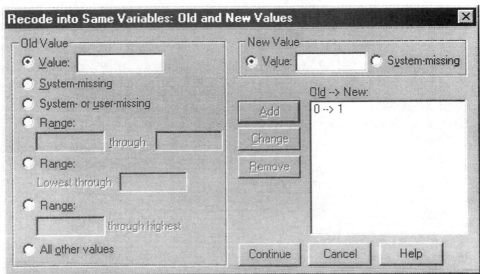

Figure 13.3   **Recode into Same Variables: Old and New Values** dialog box
to recode DUMMY for outliers.

Finally, work your way back out of the dialog boxes to yield the recode on DUMMY for outliers. To find variables discriminating identified outliers, a regression is performed on this updated variable DUMMY. Follow these SPSS commands to produce the dialog box shown in Figure 13.4. Enter DUMMY as the Dependent variable, all 44 variables as Independents, and Method is stepwise. (For convenience, you probably also want to deselect the **Save** request for Mahalanobis distance; in the **Statistics...** dialog box)

>Analyze
  >Regression
    >Linear . . .
      Dependent:
        •dummy
      Independent(s) = all 44 (exclude mah_1)

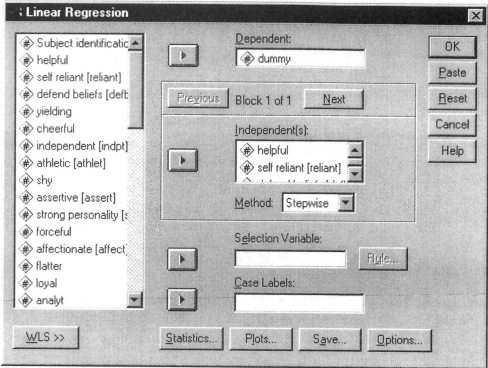

Figure 13.4   **Linear Regression** dialog box to describe outliers in factor analysis.

Clicking on the **OK** button produces *Output 13.1*.

Output 13.1. STEPWISE REGRESSION ANALYSIS TO IDENTIFY VARIABLES FOR OUTLIERS IN FACTOR ANALYSIS

[NOTE: Only selected portions of the output, particularly those showing just the final step in the regression, are shown.]

Model Summary

Model	R	R Square	Adjusted R Square	Std. Error of the Estimate
1	.252	.063	.061	.2439
2	.307	.094	.089	.2402
3	.345	.119	.112	.2372
4	.363	.132	.122	.2358
5	.383	.147	.135	.2341
6	.398	.159	.145	.2328
7	.417	.174	.158	.2309
8	.428[h]	.183	.165	.2299

h. Predictors: (Constant), self reliant, FLATTER, TRUTHFUL, act as a leader, leadership ability, FEMININE, MASCULIN, use foul language

Coefficients[a]

Model		Unstandardized Coefficients B	Std. Error	Standardized Coefficients Beta	t	Sig.
8	(Constant)	.713	.120		5.965	.000
	self reliant	-4.888E-02	.011	-.235	-4.573	.000
	FLATTER	-2.617E-02	.007	-.179	-3.691	.000
	TRUTHFUL	-5.325E-02	.015	-.174	-3.598	.000
	act as a leader	-4.539E-02	.011	-.316	-4.008	.000
	leadership ability	2.958E-02	.011	.206	2.606	.010
	FEMININE	2.914E-02	.010	.150	2.948	.003
	MASCULIN	2.439E-02	.010	.128	2.487	.013
	use foul language	-1.145E-02	.006	-.096	-2.010	.045

a. Dependent Variable: DUMMY

Excluded Variables[i]

Model		Beta In	t	Sig.	Partial Correlation	Collinearity Statistics Tolerance
8	HELPFUL	.032[h]	.603	.547	.032	.820
	defend beliefs	-.079[h]	-1.546	.123	-.081	.860
	YIELDING	-.076[h]	-1.537	.125	-.081	.921
	CHEERFUL	.072[h]	1.421	.156	.075	.876
	independent	-.024[h]	-.429	.668	-.023	.731
	athletic	.053[h]	1.069	.286	.056	.919
	SHY	-.021[h]	-.396	.692	-.021	.827
	assertive	.077[h]	1.443	.150	.076	.795
	strong personality	.055[h]	.977	.329	.051	.725
	FORCEFUL	.069[h]	1.246	.214	.066	.746
	affectionate	-.044[h]	-.809	.419	-.043	.769
	LOYAL	-.013[h]	-.256	.798	-.014	.863
	ANALYT	.034[h]	.696	.487	.037	.942
	SYMPATHY	.003[h]	.051	.960	.003	.919
	MOODY	.039[h]	.805	.421	.042	.945
	SENSITIV	-.047[h]	-.934	.351	-.049	.912
	UNDSTAND	-.021[h]	-.422	.673	-.022	.890
	compassionate	-.033[h]	-.652	.515	-.034	.907
	eager to soothe hurt feelings	.005[h]	.094	.925	.005	.899
	willing to take risks	.029[h]	.569	.570	.030	.862
	makes decisions easily	.054[h]	.981	.327	.052	.751
	self sufficient	.103[h]	1.797	.073	.094	.681
	conscientious	.053[h]	1.001	.318	.053	.797
	DOMINANT	.054[h]	.925	.355	.049	.655
	willing to take a stand	.022[h]	.402	.688	.021	.772
	HAPPY	-.070[h]	-1.342	.180	-.071	.842
	soft spoken	-.012[h]	-.227	.821	-.012	.860
	WARM	-.003[h]	-.056	.956	-.003	.820
	TENDER	-.006[h]	-.123	.902	-.006	.883
	GULLIBLE	.069[h]	1.393	.164	.073	.914
	CHILDLIK	.081[h]	1.651	.100	.087	.935

Means for the identified variables are found through the **Frequencies** or **Descriptives** procedure (Section 4.1.1). Outlying cases are deleted as shown Section 4.1.2, leaving 344 cases in the data file. (Also, you might want to delete the two created variables, mah_1 and DUMMY, from your data file.)

Information about multicollinearity is provided by squared multiple correlations (initial communalities). Follow these SPSS commands to produce the **Factor Analysis** dialog box of Figures

154

13.5 and 13.6, which lead to Output 13.2. (SPSS provides SMCs with PFA, but not with PCA.) **Scree plot** is chosen for later use.

>Analyze
    >Data Reduction
        >Factor . . .
            Variables:
                •all 44
            Extraction . . .
                Display:
                    ☑   Unrotated factor solution
                    ☑   Scree plot
                Method:
                    Principal axis factoring

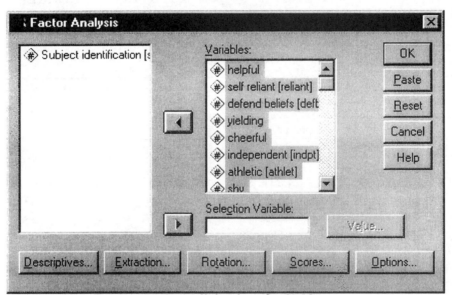

Figure 13.5   **Factor Analysis** dialog box for SMCs.

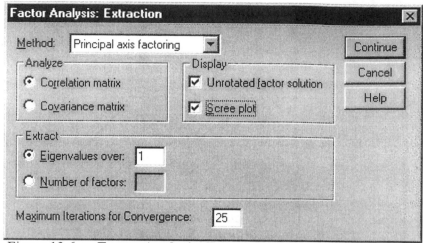

Figure 13.6   **Factor Analysis: Extraction** dialog box.

Output 13.2. **INITIAL COMMUNALITIES (SQUARED MULTIPLE CORRELATIONS) TO ASSESS MULTICOLLINEARITY, EIGENVALUES AND PROPORTIONS OF VARIANCE.**

Coefficients[a]

Model		Unstandardized Coefficients B	Std. Error	Standardized Coefficients Beta	t	Sig.
8	(Constant)	.713	.120		5.965	.000
	self reliant	-4.888E-02	.011	-.235	-4.573	.000
	FLATTER	-2.617E-02	.007	-.179	-3.691	.000
	TRUTHFUL	-5.325E-02	.015	-.174	-3.598	.000
	act as a leader	-4.539E-02	.011	-.316	-4.008	.000
	leadership ability	2.958E-02	.011	.206	2.606	.010
	FEMININE	2.914E-02	.010	.150	2.948	.003
	MASCULIN	2.439E-02	.010	.128	2.487	.013
	use foul language	-1.145E-02	.006	-.096	-2.010	.045

a. Dependent Variable: DUMMY

Information about the factorability of the correlation matrix is available by clicking on the **Descriptives...** button in the **Factor Analysis** dialog box. As seen in Figure 13.7, the **Coefficients**, **Determinant**, and **KMO** and **Bartlett's** test of sphericity are selected from the **Correlation Matrix** box, and **Univariate** descriptives are chosen from the **Statistics** box, shown in Figure 13.7. Follow these SPSS commands. Selected output from this procedure is displayed in *Output 13.3*.

>Descriptives . . .
Statistics
☑ Univariate descriptives
☑ Initial Solutions
Correlation Matrix
☑ Coefficients
☑ Determinant
☑ KMO and Bartlett's test of sphericity

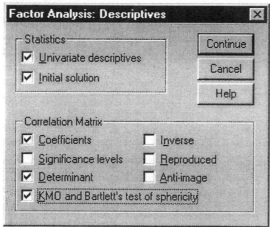

Figure 13.7   **Factor Analysis: Descriptives**
for main analysis.

Output 13.3. **DESCRIPTIVE STATISTICS AND INFORMATION ABOUT FACTORABILITY OF CORRELATION MATRIX FOR FACTOR ANALYSIS.**

Descriptive Statistics

	Mean	Std. Deviation	Analysis N
HELPFUL	6.07	.96	344
self reliant	6.01	1.03	344
defend beliefs	5.98	1.21	344
YIELDING	4.56	1.25	344
CHEERFUL	5.83	1.00	344
independent	5.91	1.26	344
athletic	3.66	1.91	344
SHY	2.97	1.56	344
assertive	4.67	1.42	344
strong personality	5.11	1.47	344
FORCEFUL	3.97	1.66	344
affectionate	5.98	1.09	344
FLATTER	4.51	1.66	344
LOYAL	6.62	.64	344
ANALYT	5.38	1.50	344
FEMININE	5.58	1.23	344
SYMPATHY	5.99	1.06	344
MOODY	3.17	1.59	344
SENSITIV	5.85	1.07	344
UNDSTAND	5.93	.92	344
compassionate	5.88	.95	344
leadership ability	4.65	1.71	344
eager to soothe hurt feelings	5.80	1.16	344
willing to take risks	4.19	1.63	344

Correlation Matrix[a]

		HELPFUL	self reliant	defend beliefs	YIELDING	CHEERFUL
Correlation	HELPFUL	1.000	.337	.239	.114	.220
	self reliant	.337	1.000	.145	-.012	.247
	defend beliefs	.239	.145	1.000	-.078	.102
	YIELDING	.114	-.012	-.078	1.000	.181
	CHEERFUL	.220	.247	.102	.181	1.000
	independent	.271	.514	.211	-.034	.186
	athletic	.173	.147	.066	.053	.181
	SHY	-.138	-.114	-.239	.010	-.185
	assertive	.177	.301	.280	-.107	.176
	strong personality	.218	.240	.275	-.093	.173
	FORCEFUL	.070	.173	.297	-.175	.002
	affectionate	.349	.104	.297	.086	.270
	FLATTER	.065	-.056	.096	.112	.155
	LOYAL	.314	.153	.268	.066	.284
	ANALYT	.148	.173	.221	-.081	-.015
	FEMININE	.153	.185	.046	.197	.201
	SYMPATHY	.163	.070	.125	.124	.117
	MOODY	-.119	-.159	.052	-.067	-.332
	SENSITIV	.176	.097	.137	.106	.134
	individualistic	.215	.299	.184	-.080	.133
	use foul language	.017	.036	-.002	-.007	.027
	love children	.198	.001	.125	.181	.175
	competitive	.153	.147	.151	-.020	.081
	ambitious	.190	.232	.168	.046	.083
	GENTLE	.232	.093	.115	.201	.308

a. Determinant = 1.271E-08

KMO and Bartlett's Test

Kaiser-Meyer-Olkin Measure of Sampling Adequacy.		.852
Bartlett's Test of Sphericity	Approx. Chi-Square	5954.218
	df	946
	Sig.	.000

13.2   PRINCIPAL FACTORS ANALYSIS

13.2.1   Principal Factors Extraction with Varimax Rotation

With SPSS, information about initial eigenvalues and proportion of variance is available from the same PFA run that provides information about multicollinearity (*Output 13.2*). The Scree Plot requested earlier (cf. Figure 13.6) is reproduced in Figure 13.8, below.

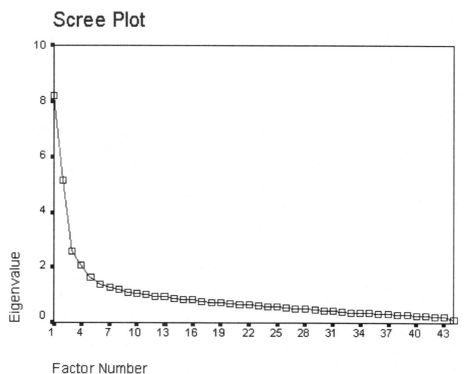

Figure 13.8   Scree plot.

The Factor Analysis for the PFA run with 4 factors and Varimax rotation is shown earlier in Figure 13.5 (corresponding to Table 13.19 in *Using Multivariate Statistics*), Clicking on the **Extraction...** button brings up the **Factor Analysis: Extraction** dialog box displayed in Figure 13.9 in which the **Number of factors** chosen is 4 and **Method** selected remains **Principal-axis factoring**. Request for **Display** of the **Unrotated factor solution** provides final communalities and proportions of variances accounted for by the four factors.

160

```
>Analyze
    >Data Reduction
        Factor
            Extraction
                Method:  Principal axis factoring
                    Display
                        ☑ Unrotated factor solution
                    Extract
                        ⊙ Number of factors  =  4
```

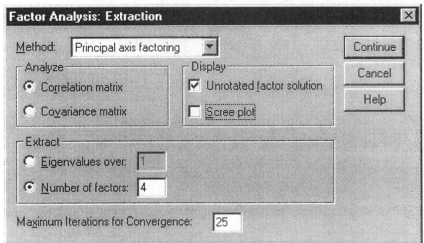

Figure 13.9   **Factor Analysis: Extraction** dialog box for four factors.

Clicking on the **Continue** button returns the **Factor** dialog box, where clicking on the
Descriptives... button brings up the **Factor Analysis: Descriptives** dialog box of Figure 13.10.

```
>Descriptives
    Statistics:
        ☑ Initial solution
```

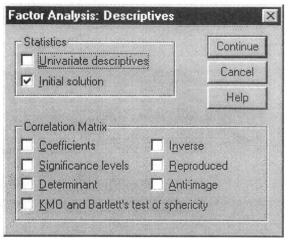

Figure 13.10   **Factor Analysis: Descriptives**
for main analysis.

Note that only the **Initial Solution** statistics (default) are chosen.

Clicking on the **Continue** button returns the **Factor Analysis** dialog box, in which clicking on the **Rotation...** button produces the **Factor Analysis: Rotation** dialog box in Figure 13.11. **Varimax** is chosen as the **Method**, with request for **Display** of **Rotated Solution** and **Loading Plot(s)**.

Rotation . . .
    Method
        ⊙Varimax
    Display
        ☑ Rotated solution
        ☑ Loading Plots

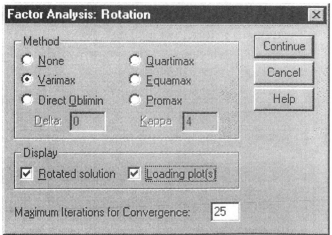

Figure 13.11   **Factor Analysis: Rotation** dialog
box for Varimax rotation.

Clicking on the **Continue** button returns the **Factor Analysis** dialog box. From here, clicking on the **Options...** button brings up the **Factor Analysis: Options** dialog box (Figure 13.12), in which a request is made that **Coefficient Display Format** be **Sorted by size** and to **Suppress absolute values less than** .25. These actions make the output much easier to read and interpret.

Options . . .
    Coefficient Display Format
        ☑ Sorted by size
        ☑ Suppress absolute values less than .25

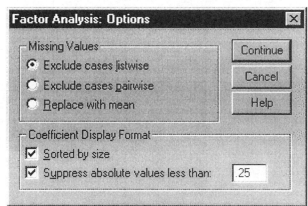

Figure 13.12   **Factor Analysis: Options**
                  dialog box.

Clicking on the **Continue** button returns the **Factor Analysis** dialog box, where clicking on **OK** produces *Output 13.4*. SPSS does not provide SMCs of each factor with the variables. The 3-D plot of factors 1, 2, and 3 (shown in Figure 13.13) is interesting, but by further manipulation it can reveal much more about the data (cf. description below).

Output 13.4. **PRINCIPAL FACTOR ANALYSIS. PARTIAL OUTPUT.**

Communalities

	Initial	Extraction
HELPFUL	.374	.282
self reliant	.461	.398
defend beliefs	.417	.249
YIELDING	.230	.151
CHEERFUL	.492	.360
independent	.538	.454
athletic	.258	.184
SHY	.325	.157
assertive	.538	.440
strong personality	.593	.507
FORCEFUL	.566	.464
affectionate	.553	.480
FLATTER	.296	.200
LOYAL	.391	.294
ANALYT	.242	.151
FEMININE	.358	.156
SYMPATHY	.453	.441
MOODY	.381	.271
SENSITIV	.486	.444
UNDSTAND	.617	.581
compassionate	.649	.685
leadership ability	.763	.577
eager to soothe hurt feelings	.435	.388
willing to take risks	.422	.276
makes decisions easily	.489	.376
self sufficient	.633	.636
conscientious	.399	.350
DOMINANT	.562	.540
MASCULIN	.316	.189

Total Variance Explained

	Initial Eigenvalues			Extraction Sums of Squared Loadings			Rotation Sums of Squared Loadings		
Factor	Total	% of Variance	Cumulative %	Total	% of Variance	Cumulative %	Total	% of Variance	Cumulative %
1	8.194	18.623	18.623	7.619	17.317	17.317	6.014	13.668	13.668
2	5.154	11.713	30.335	4.601	10.457	27.774	4.003	9.097	22.765
3	2.590	5.887	36.223	1.958	4.449	32.223	3.400	7.726	30.491
4	2.073	4.711	40.934	1.465	3.329	35.552	2.227	5.060	35.552

Rotated Factor Matrix[a]

	Factor			
	1	2	3	4
leadership ability	.739			
act as a leader	.727			
strong personality	.701			
DOMINANT	.675		-.281	
FORCEFUL	.645			
assertive	.643			
willing to take a stand	.593			
competitive	.541			
willing to take risks	.496			
makes decisions easily	.483			.345
ambitious	.466			
individualistic	.435			
defend beliefs	.413	.280		
SHY	-.383			
athletic	.324			
HELPFUL	.311	.270	.296	
MASCULIN	.308		-.287	
ANALYT	.277			
compassionate		.811		
UNDSTAND		.731		
SENSITIV		.660		
SYMPATHY		.649		
eager to soothe hurt feelings		.540	.297	
affectionate	.300	.392	.391	-.289
LOYAL		.388	.319	

Factor Transformation Matrix

Factor	1	2	3	4
1	.735	.508	.399	.207
2	-.619	.541	.541	-.176
3	.233	.243	-.270	-.902
4	.152	-.624	.689	-.336

Extraction Method: Principal Axis Factoring.
Rotation Method: Varimax with Kaiser Normalization.

Factor Plot in Rotated Factor Space

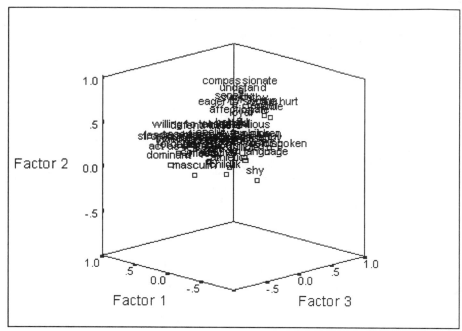

Figure 13.13   3-D plot of factors 1, 2 and 3.

Better views of the factor loading plots are available in SPSS by double clicking on the plot "Factor Plot in Rotated Factor Space," which activates the SPSS Chart Editor, where many manipulations can be made. In the Chart Editor, clicking on the **3-D Rotation** button, an icon that looks like an inverted Y, allows you to spin the 3-D plot. An example showing factor 1 vs. factor 2 is displayed in Figure 13.14.

Factor Plot in Rotated Factor Space

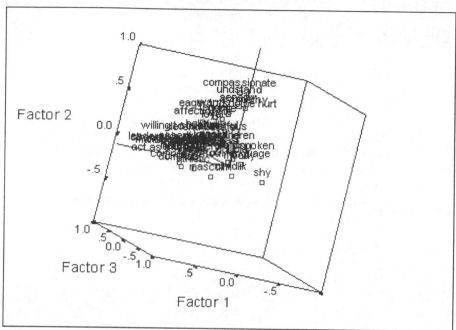

Figure 13.14   Rotated 3-D plot.

Other loading plots (e.g., factor 1 vs. factor 4) can be produced using the syntax editor produced by clicking on the **Paste** button in the **Factor Analysis** dialog box, bringing up the syntax editor. The request for factor loading plots 1 vs. 4 is typed in, as per Figure 13.15: /PLOT ROTATION (1,4). The result is displayed in Figure 13.16.

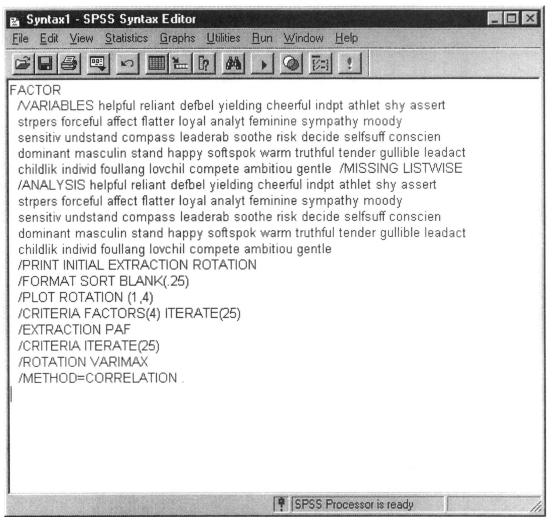

Figure 13.15   Syntax box for plot of factor 1 versus factor 4.

168

Factor Plot in Rotated Factor Space

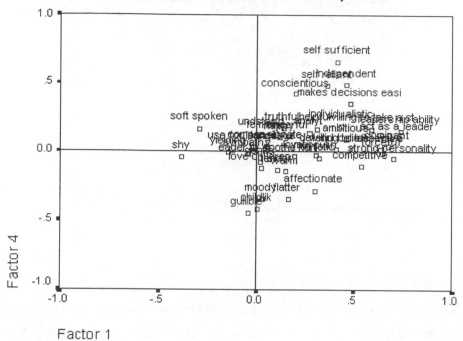

Factor 1

Figure 13.16   Plot of loading of variables on factors 1 and 4.

13.2.2 Oblique Rotation and Factor Score Plots

Oblique rotation is accomplished by clicking on the **Rotation...** button of the **Factor Analysis** dialog box, producing the **Factor Analysis: Rotation** dialog box, where **Promax** is chosen as the **Method** with **Kappa:** of 4, as seen in Figure 13.17.

Rotation
    Method
          ⊙ Promax, Kappa = 4
    Display
          ☑ Rotated solution

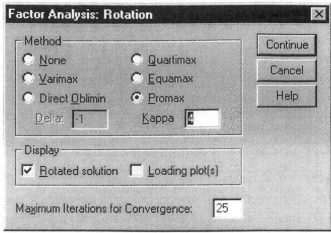

Figure 13.17   **Factor Analysis: Rotation** dialog box
showing oblique rotation.

Clicking on the **Continue** button returns the **Factor Analysis** dialog box, where clicking on the **OK** button produces the oblique rotated solution and the factor correlation matrix in *Output 13.5*. Note that the Promax solution differs from the quartimin solution demonstrated in *Using Multivariate Statistics*.

Output 13.5. **CORRELATIONS AMONG FACTORS FOLLOWING PROMAX ROTATION. PARTIAL OUTPUT**

Factor Correlation Matrix

Factor	1	2	3	4
1	1.000	.247	.211	.265
2	.247	1.000	.528	2.172E-03
3	.211	.528	1.000	4.112E-02
4	.265	2.172E-03	4.112E-02	1.000

Extraction Method: Principal Axis Factoring.
Rotation Method: Promax with Kaiser Normalization.

SPSS FACTOR does not directly provide scatterplots of factor scores. Instead, factor scores are saved, and then plotted through the scatterplot procedure. Clicking on the **Scores...** button of the **Factor Analysis** dialog box brings up the **Factor Analysis: Factor Scores** dialog box of Figure 13.18.

170

>Scores…
      ☑ Save as Variables
      Method
            ⊙ Regression

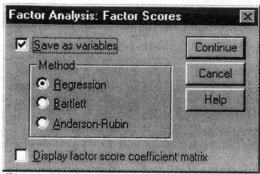

Figure 13.18   **Factor Analysis: Factor Scores dialog** box.

Clicking on **Save as variables** box and **Regression** in the **Method** box (and then the **Continue** and **OK** buttons) adds scores for the four factors to the data set, as seen in Figure 13.19.

	ambitiou	gentle	fac1_1	fac2_1	fac3_1	fac4_1
1	7	7	.48910	1.14445	1.72525	.73211
2	4	4	-1.32257	-1.54693	-1.47051	-.80198
3	4	5	-1.02602	-.31484	-.20695	.76763
4	6	5	-.55103	-.12222	-.04359	.46630
5	7	7	1.76362	1.11304	.86864	-.54524
6	5	6	-1.06784	-.30192	-.06931	1.31757
7	1	5	-1.97205	.02604	-.75536	-1.80625
8	4	6	.65965	.46215	.27414	.51827

Figure 13.19   Factor scores added to data set.

Choosing **Graphs** menu and then **Scatter...** produces the **Scatterplot** dialog box (cf. Figure 4.8). Choosing **Simple** and clicking on the **Define** button produces the **Simple Scatterplot** dialog box of Figure 13.20, in which the variables chosen are fac2_1 for the **Y Axis:** and fac4_1 for the **X Axis:**

(factors 2 and 4 are the most highly uncorrelated in *Output 13.5*). Figure 13.21 presents the scatterplot for scores of these two distinct factors.

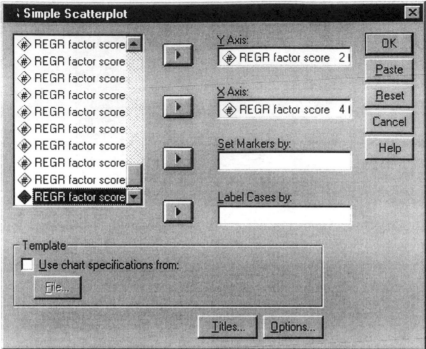

Figure 13.20   **Simple Scatterplot** dialog box for factor score plot.

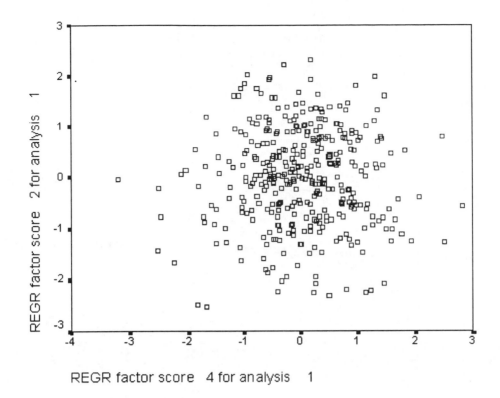

Figure 13.21   Scatterplot of scores for factors 2 and 4.

Chapter 14. Structural Equation Modeling

This chapter demonstrates structural equation modeling using AMOS 4.0 program (SmallWaters, Inc.), for the complete example of Chapter 14 of *UMS*. The files to use are WISCSEM.sav and HLTHSEM.sav. (See Section 3.1 of Chapter 3 for detailed information on obtaining the SPSS files.)

The AMOS program uses a different interface than that of SPSS, although there are many similarities. To persons already familiar with accessing features in SPSS, navigating AMOS will not be difficult. Still, AMOS has many unique commands that must be learned. AMOS is available in two formats: as an add-in to SPSS (where it is accessed through the **Analyze** menu of SPSS, as an additional SPSS procedure), or as a stand-alone program (here, it must be launched independently, as any other program). In either format, the interface is identical.

14.1   THE AMOS GRAPHICS ENVIRONMENT

Models may be specified and analyzed in AMOS through syntax (called Amos Basic Commands) or path diagrams and menu choices. The latter approach is taken here. Immediately upon opening the program, you will notice that the main AMOS Graphics screen (shown in Figure 14.1) consists of two windows. The right-hand window has two parts, a blank drawing page on the right and a components list on the left. On the drawing page, you create a diagram that represents your model. The components list is useful information about your model, such as the status of the run, files available, and more. The components list changes to appropriate features as your model progresses.

The left-hand window is a graphics toolbar with various icons for tools used to create and manipulate objects in the drawing page. First, you select a tool and then you use it in the drawing page.

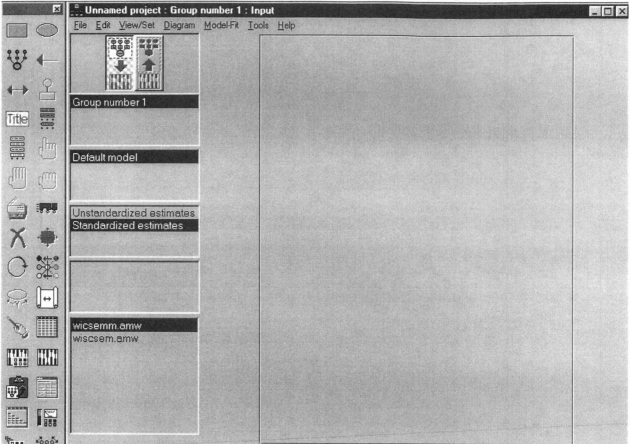

Figure 14.1   The two windows of the main AMOS graphics screen.

14.2   EVALUATION OF ASSUMPTIONS

Missing data, normality, and outliers are assessed through SPSS as per Section 4.1.1 and 4.1.6. Alternatively, normality and multivariate outliers (Mahalanobis distance) may be assessed by requesting normality and outlier tests as part of the initial AMOS analysis. As a convenience, outliers are omitted from both the WISCSEM.sav and HLTHSEM.sav data sets

Plots to evaluate linearity are produced as per Section 4.1.4. Convergence of the program assures a nonsingular covariance matrix. Residuals are assessed by requesting them as part of the model run.

14.3   CONFIRMATORY FACTOR ANALYSIS

The first example demonstrates confirmatory factor analysis of 11 subtests of the Wechsler Intelligence Scale for Children (WISC) in a sample of learning-disabled children. Your initial task when using AMOS is to link the SPSS data set to the AMOS program. Do this by executing the following commands, which give one entrée the **Data File** dialog box shown in Figure 14.2.

```
>File
    >Data File...  (alternatively: Ctrl + D)
        File Name
            Open
```

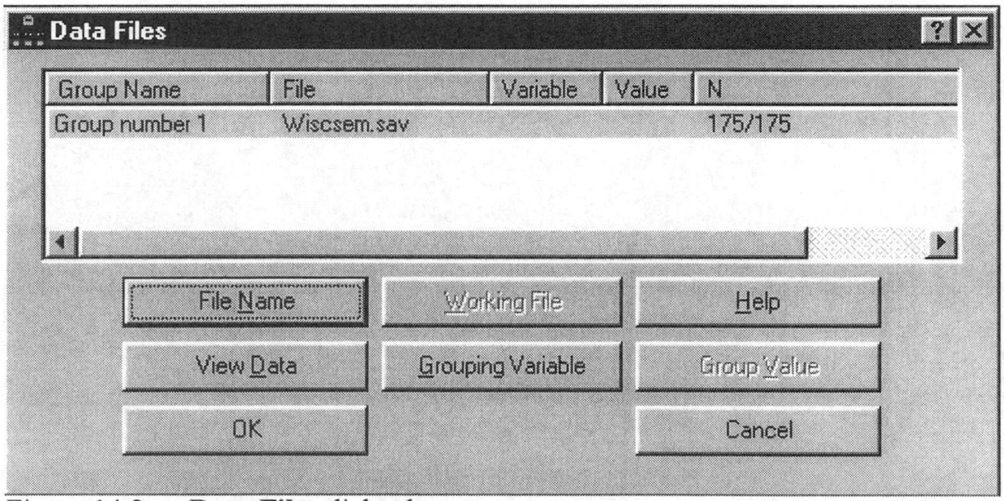

Figure 14.2   **Data Files** dialog box.

Now, from the **Data Files** dialog box, click the **File Name** pushbutton and navigate to the location (directory or folder) of WISCSEM.sav on you computer. Select the SPSS data file by clicking on it once to highlight it. Then, click the **Open** pushbutton, which returns you to the AMOS **Data Files** dialog box with the file name listed (cf. Figure 14.2). Finally, click the pushbutton **OK**. The WISCSEM data set is now loaded into AMOS and ready for your manipulation. If you click the **View Data** pushbutton in the **Data Files** dialog box, the SPSS program is launched and it opens the WISCSEM.sav data set.

14.3.1 Model Specification for CFA

Begin your model by drawing an observed variable. In AMOS, observed variables are represented by a box. (Unobserved variables are represented by an elipise). Select the square box (first icon, upper left, on the toolbar), and then, while continuing to hold down the left mouse button, go to the drawing page and draw the box. (Alternatively, one may choose an item from the **Diagram** main menu.) Once an object is created, it can be maniplated by clicking on a particular object in the drawing page and then on one of the icons in the tool bar. For example, to move an object, first select it in the drawing page, and then on the toolbar icon click on the icon that looks like a truck (7th object down in the right, as seen in Figure 14.3). Objects can be resized by clicking on the icon that is a square with bi-directional arrows on all four sides (8th object down, just below the truck, right-hand side of the two-column toolbar).

Figure 14.3 shows creation of a box for an observed variable.

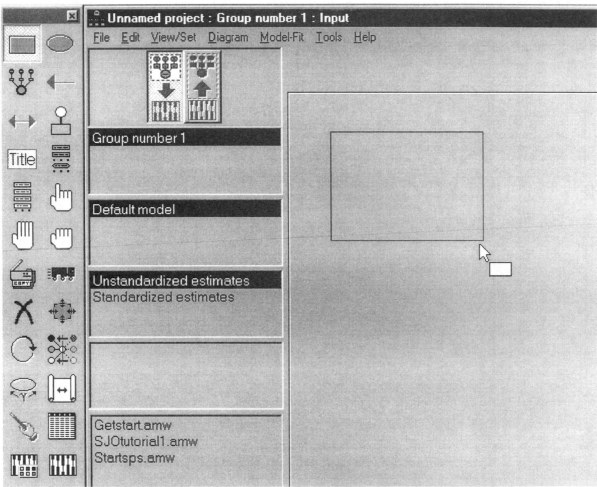

Figure 14.3   AMOS graphics screen with box for creating ordered variable shown by arrow.

After double-clicking on the variable box produces the **Object Properties** dialog box, choosing

Text (tab)
      Variable name
            •info
      Variable label
            •information

Figure 14.4 shows the **Object Properties** dialog box filled in.

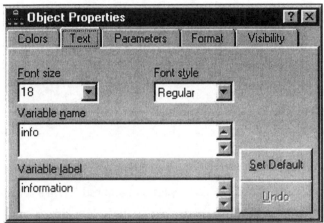

Figure 14.4   **Object Properties** dialog box.

The **Variable name** must be a variable in the data set. The **Variable label** is what appears in the box on the diagram.

Once all the boxes and ellipses are filled in and positioned, arrows are drawn to show relationships. Arrors are formed by choosing either the single-headed arrow (to draw a path between variables) or the double-headed arrow (to represent covariances) icon from the graphics toolbar, and holding down the mouse button while moving from one object to another. The single arrow points to the object where the button is released, as seen in Figure 14.5.

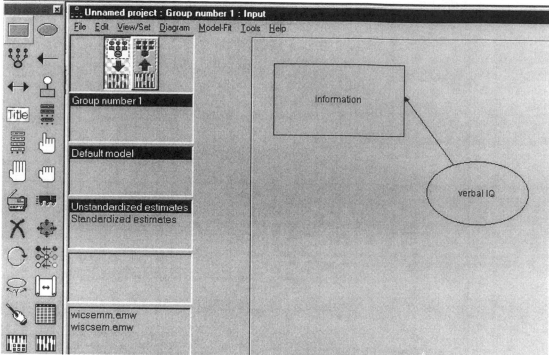

Figure 14.5   Creating a path between a latent (unobserved) variable and a measured (observed) variable.

Figure 14.6 shows the completed path diagram. Note that all paths between error and other variables must explicitly be set to 1, and that errors are considered latent variables for purposes of diagramming.

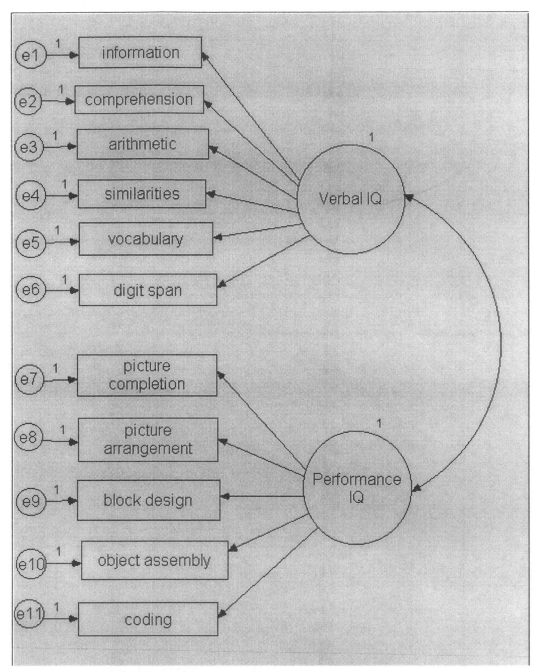

Figure 14.6   Hypothesized CFA model.

14.3.2 CFA Model Estimation and Preliminary Evaluation

Output options are selected before a model is run by choosing these AMOS commands.

>View/Set
   >Analysis Properties...
     Output (tab)
      ☑Standardized estimates
      ☑Squared multiple correlations
      ☑Residual moments
      ☑Modification indices

Figure 14.7 displays options selected in the **Analysis Properties** dialog box, following the above commands. Note that the **Output** tab is selected. **Tests for normality and outliers** are not requested here because these issues have already been addressed.

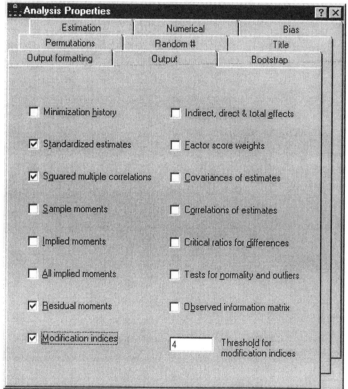

Figure 14.7   **Analysis Properties** dialog box with
                 Output tab shown.

The remaining tabs may be ignored if default settings are to be used, such as maximum likelihood estimation. Other choices are available under the **Estimation** tab.

Clicking on the "⊠" symbol in the upper right of the window closes it. The model is run by choosing

>M̲odel-Fit
>C̲alculate Estimates

This results in a notice that output is being written, a chi-square value is shown, and a notice that the run has finished, as seen in Figure 14.8.

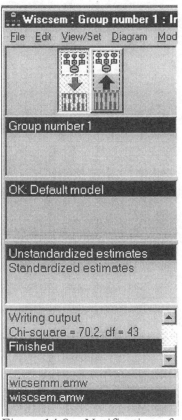

Figure 14.8   Notification of a
successful run.

Output in table format is accessed by choosing

>View/Set
    >Table Output

This produces a window in which the diagram is shown, and the components of the results are listed on the left, as seen in Figure 14.9.

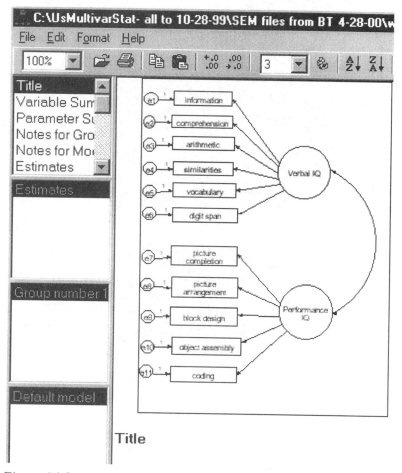

Figure 14.9   Table output window with components listed on the left.

Clicking on each component brings it into the display at the right. We start with **Variable Summary** and continue through the remaining components to **Fit Measures 1 and 2**. Selected results are shown in *Output 14.1*.

Your model contains the following variables

info	observed	endogenous
comp	observed	endogenous
arith	observed	endogenous
simil	observed	endogenous
vocab	observed	endogenous
digit	observed	endogenous
pictcomp	observed	endogenous
parang	observed	endogenous
block	observed	endogenous
object	observed	endogenous
coding	observed	endogenous
Performance_IQ	unobserved	exogenous
Verbal IQ	unobserved	exogenous
e1	unobserved	exogenous
e2	unobserved	exogenous
e3	unobserved	exogenous
e4	unobserved	exogenous
e5	unobserved	exogenous
e6	unobserved	exogenous
e7	unobserved	exogenous
e8	unobserved	exogenous
e9	unobserved	exogenous
e10	unobserved	exogenous
e11	unobserved	exogenous

Number of variables in your model:	24
Number of observed variables:	11
Number of unobserved variables:	13
Number of exogenous variables:	13
Number of endogenous variables:	11

Summary of Parameters

	Weights	Covariances	Variances	Means	Intercepts	Total
Fixed	11	0	2	0	0	13
Labeled	0	0	0	0	0	0
Unlabeled	11	1	11	0	0	23
Total	22	1	13	0	0	36

The model is recursive.

Sample size = 175

Computation of degrees of freedom

    Number of distinct sample moments = 66
    Number of distinct parameters to be estimated = 23
    Degrees of freedom = 66 - 23 = 43

Minimum was achieved

Chi-square = 70.236
Degrees of freedom = 43
Probability level = 0.005

Regression Weights

			Estimate	S.E.	C.R.	P	Label
info	<—	Verbal IQ	2.206	0.201	10.997	0.000	
comp	<—	Verbal IQ	2.042	0.211	9.682	0.000	
arith	<—	Verbal IQ	1.300	0.173	7.534	0.000	
simil	<—	Verbal IQ	2.232	0.225	9.911	0.000	
vocab	<—	Verbal IQ	2.250	0.201	11.193	0.000	
digit	<—	Verbal IQ	1.053	0.213	4.952	0.000	
pictcomp	<—	Performance_IQ	1.742	0.243	7.166	0.000	
parang	<—	Performance_IQ	1.253	0.225	5.566	0.000	
block	<—	Performance_IQ	1.846	0.223	8.287	0.000	
object	<—	Performance_IQ	1.605	0.237	6.780	0.000	
coding	<—	Performance_IQ	0.207	0.255	0.811	0.417	

Standardized Regression Weights

			Estimate
info	<—	Verbal IQ	0.760
comp	<—	Verbal IQ	0.691
arith	<—	Verbal IQ	0.565
simil	<—	Verbal IQ	0.703
vocab	<—	Verbal IQ	0.770
digit	<—	Verbal IQ	0.390
pictcomp	<—	Performance_IQ	0.595
parang	<—	Performance_IQ	0.473
block	<—	Performance_IQ	0.683
object	<—	Performance_IQ	0.566
coding	<—	Performance_IQ	0.072

Covariances

			Estimate	S.E.	C.R.	P	Label
Performance_IQ	<—>	Verbal IQ	0.589	0.076	7.792	0.000	

Correlations

			Estimate
Performance_IQ	<—>	Verbal IQ	0.589

Variances

	Estimate	S.E.	C.R.	P	Label
Verbal IQ	1.000				
Performance_IQ	1.000				
e1	3.566	0.508	7.014	0.000	
e2	4.572	0.587	7.793	0.000	
e3	3.602	0.421	8.547	0.000	
e4	5.096	0.663	7.680	0.000	
e5	3.487	0.508	6.866	0.000	
e6	6.162	0.682	9.030	0.000	
e7	5.526	0.760	7.276	0.000	
e8	5.463	0.660	8.275	0.000	
e9	3.894	0.642	6.066	0.000	
e10	5.467	0.721	7.578	0.000	
e11	8.159	0.877	9.309	0.000	

Squared Multiple Correlations

	Estimate
coding	0.005
object	0.320
block	0.467
parang	0.223
pictcomp	0.354
digit	0.152
vocab	0.592
simil	0.494
arith	0.319
comp	0.477
info	0.577

Residual Covariances

	coding	object	block	parang	pictcomp	digit	vocab	simil	arith	comp	info
coding	0.000	0.098	0.445	0.028	-0.962	1.208	0.563	-0.642	0.436	0.265	-0.210
object	0.098	0.000	0.097	-0.106	0.219	-0.729	-0.589	0.310	-0.948	0.773	-0.562
block	0.445	0.097	0.000	0.204	-0.195	-0.614	-0.096	-0.184	0.279	0.729	-0.600
parang	0.028	-0.106	0.204	0.000	-0.253	0.283	-0.636	0.863	0.424	-0.044	-0.076
pictcomp	-0.962	0.219	-0.195	-0.253	0.000	-0.486	0.134	1.140	-0.288	1.425	-0.310
digit	1.208	-0.729	-0.614	0.283	-0.486	0.000	-0.049	-0.128	0.300	-0.270	0.382
vocab	0.563	-0.589	-0.096	-0.636	0.134	-0.049	0.000	-0.030	-0.320	-0.002	0.343
simil	-0.642	0.310	-0.184	0.863	1.140	-0.128	-0.030	0.000	-0.204	0.230	-0.194
arith	0.436	-0.948	0.279	0.424	-0.288	0.300	-0.320	-0.204	0.000	0.014	0.435
comp	0.265	0.773	0.729	-0.044	1.425	-0.270	-0.002	0.230	0.014	0.000	-0.494
info	-0.210	-0.562	-0.600	-0.076	-0.310	0.382	0.343	-0.194	0.435	-0.494	0.000

Standardized Residual Covariances

	coding	object	block	parang	pictcomp	digit	vocab	simil	arith	comp	info
coding	0.000	0.159	0.758	0.049	-1.513	2.062	0.886	-0.931	0.872	0.413	-0.333
object	0.159	0.000	0.156	-0.180	0.331	-1.248	-0.908	0.443	-1.884	1.186	-0.872
block	0.758	0.156	0.000	0.358	-0.301	-1.098	-0.152	-0.272	0.576	1.159	-0.965
parang	0.049	-0.180	0.358	0.000	-0.414	0.519	-1.058	1.327	0.905	-0.073	-0.127
pictcomp	-1.513	0.331	-0.301	-0.414	0.000	-0.805	0.199	1.573	-0.553	2.112	-0.464
digit	2.062	-1.248	-1.098	0.519	-0.805	0.000	-0.079	-0.191	0.623	-0.431	0.618
vocab	0.886	-0.908	-0.152	-1.058	0.199	-0.079	0.000	-0.037	-0.575	-0.002	0.460
simil	-0.931	0.443	-0.272	1.327	1.573	-0.191	-0.037	0.000	-0.343	0.291	-0.245
arith	0.872	-1.884	0.576	0.905	-0.553	0.623	-0.575	-0.343	0.000	0.025	0.790
comp	0.413	1.186	1.159	-0.073	2.112	-0.431	-0.002	0.291	0.025	0.000	-0.672
info	-0.333	-0.872	-0.965	-0.127	-0.464	0.618	0.460	-0.245	0.790	-0.672	0.000

Modification Indices

Covariances:

	M.I.	Par Change
e7 <--> e11	4.221	-1.137
e6 <--> e11	4.897	1.207
e5 <--> e8	4.059	-0.785
e3 <--> e10	6.280	-0.938
e2 <--> Performance_IQ	8.955	0.561
e2 <--> e7	4.581	0.953

Variances:

	M.I.	Par Change

Regression Weights:

	M.I.	Par Change
coding <- digit	4.509	0.171
object <- arith	5.513	-0.194
pictcomp <- coding	4.194	-0.138
digit <- coding	4.608	0.143
vocab <- parang	4.065	-0.122
arith <- object	4.276	-0.109
comp <- Performance_IQ	4.569	0.438
comp <- object	5.317	0.142
comp <- pictcomp	7.109	0.159

Fit Measures

Fit Measure	Default model	Saturated	Independence	Macro
Discrepancy	70.236	0.000	516.237	CMIN
Degrees of freedom	43	0	55	DF
P	0.005		0.000	P
Number of parameters	23	66	11	NPAR
Discrepancy / df	1.633		9.386	CMINDF
RMR	0.466	0.000	2.241	RMR
GFI	0.931	1.000	0.527	GFI
Adjusted GFI	0.894		0.432	AGFI
Parsimony-adjusted GFI	0.606		0.439	PGFI
Normed fit index	0.864	1.000	0.000	NFI
Relative fit index	0.826		0.000	RFI
Incremental fit index	0.942	1.000	0.000	IFI
Tucker-Lewis index	0.924		0.000	TLI
Comparative fit index	0.941	1.000	0.000	CFI
Parsimony ratio	0.782	0.000	1.000	PRATIO
Parsimony-adjusted NFI	0.675	0.000	0.000	PNFI
Parsimony-adjusted CFI	0.736	0.000	0.000	PCFI
Noncentrality parameter estimate	27.236	0.000	461.237	NCP
NCP lower bound	8.130	0.000	392.198	NCPLO
NCP upper bound	54.240	0.000	537.736	NCPHI
FMIN	0.404	0.000	2.967	FMIN
F0	0.157	0.000	2.651	F0
F0 lower bound	0.047	0.000	2.254	F0LO
F0 upper bound	0.312	0.000	3.090	F0HI
RMSEA	0.060		0.220	RMSEA
RMSEA lower bound	0.033		0.202	RMSEALO
RMSEA upper bound	0.085		0.237	RMSEAHI
P for test of close fit	0.239		0.000	PCLOSE
Akaike information criterion (AIC)	116.236	132.000	538.237	AIC
Browne-Cudeck criterion	119.643	141.778	539.867	BCC
Bayes information criterion	244.178	499.137	599.427	BIC
Consistent AIC	212.026	406.876	584.050	CAIC
Expected cross validation index	0.668	0.759	3.093	ECVI
ECVI lower bound	0.558	0.759	2.697	ECVILO
ECVI upper bound	0.823	0.759	3.533	ECVIHI
MECVI	0.688	0.815	3.103	MECVI
Hoelter .05 index	147		25	HFIVE
Hoelter .01 index	168		28	HONE

Fit Measures

	CMIN	DF	P	NPAR	CMINDF	RMR	GFI	AGFI	PGFI	NFI
Default model	70.236	43	0.005	23	1.633	0.466	0.931	0.894	0.606	0.864
Saturated	0.000	0		66		0.000	1.000			1.000
Independence	516.237	55	0.000	11	9.386	2.241	0.527	0.432	0.439	0.000

The original (input) covariance matrix is not shown. The output begins with an indication of observed and latent variables, and whether each variable is an IV (exogenous) or a DV (endogenous).

Summary of Parameters permits a check that parameters are free or estimated as intended. **Fit Measures** are consistent with those of Table 14.16 in *UMS*. **Standard Residuals** are available in table form, but are not plotted. These are somewhat different from those in Table 14.17 of *UMS*; in general they tend to be smaller (note that variables in the matrix are reversed – the first, INFO, is listed last).

Squared Multiple Correlations are identical to those of Table 14.19 in *UMS*. The table labeled **Regression Weights** shows **Estimates** and **S.E.**s (standard errors) that diverge a bit from those of Table 14.18 in *UMS*. These are unstandardized values, and the ones in Table 14.18 are partially standardized. However, the tests for those values, **C.R = Estimate/S.E.**, produce the same values as the *z* tests in Table 14.18. The **Standardized Regression Weights** are identical to the complete standardized solution of Table 14.18.

A diagram of the final CFA model before modifications is produced by clicking on the up-arrow icon on the main AMOS Graphics screen, as seen in Figure 14.10.

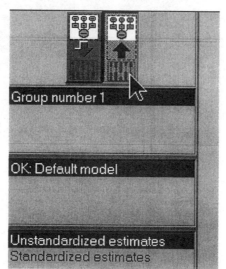

Figure 14.10   Request to show diagram
with standardized weights.

This produces Figure 14.11.

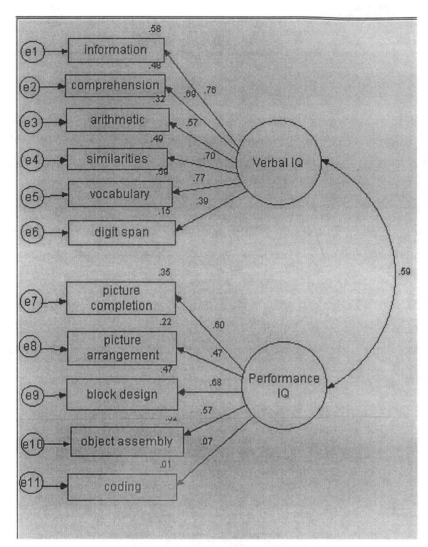

Figure 14.11   Final CFA model before modifications.

The diagram shows standardized regression and correlation coefficients. The value that appears above each observed variable is 1 error variance. For example, e1 = 1 - .58 = .42. Thus, the .58 can be interpreted as standardized non-error variance for the observed variable, information.

14.3.3 Model Modification

Modification Indices for Regression Weights: in *Output 14.1* are different from those in the various matrices of (unstandardized) modification indices of Table 14.20 in *UMS*. For example, the modification index for the path between CODING and DIGIT here is 4.509; in Table 14.20 it is 4.899. Looking exclusively at the modification indices between observed and unobserved variables, the only path that appears is between COMP and Performance IQ. This is consistent with the large MI between e2 (the error for COMP) and Performance IQ.

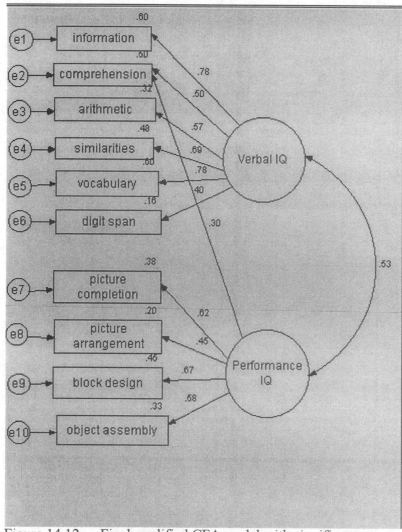

Figure 14.12   Final modified CFA model with significant
coefficients presented in standardized form.

The model is rerun as per Figures 14.6 through 14.9. Figure 14.12 shows the final modified model.

14.4   SEM

Figure 14.13 shows the hypothesized SEM model created through AMOS using techniques described in Section 14.2.1.

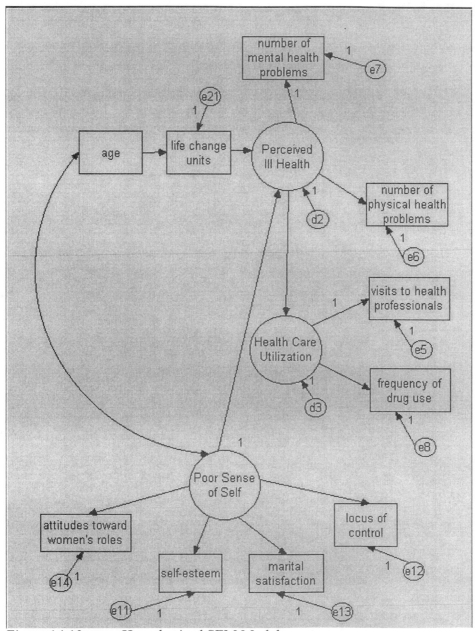

Figure 14.13   Hypothesized SEM Model.

194

14.4.1   SEM Model Estimation and Preliminary Evaluation

Output options are shown Figure 14.14. Note that AMOS does not provide robust statistics. One might want to consider transforming the poorly distributed variable: TIMEDRS, PHYHEAL, MENHEAL, DRUGUSE, ESTEEM, CONTROL, and ATTMAR. No transformation is done here to keep output as close as possible to that of *UMS*.

>View/Set
    >Analysis Properties...
        Output (tab)
            ☑   Standardized estimates
            ☑   Squared multiple correlations
            ☑   Residual moments
            ☑   Modification indices
            ☑   Tests for normality and outliers

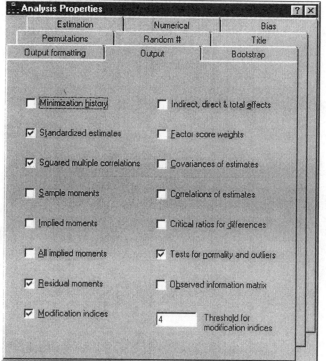

Figure 14.14   **AMOS Analysis Properties** dialog box
with **Output** options shown.

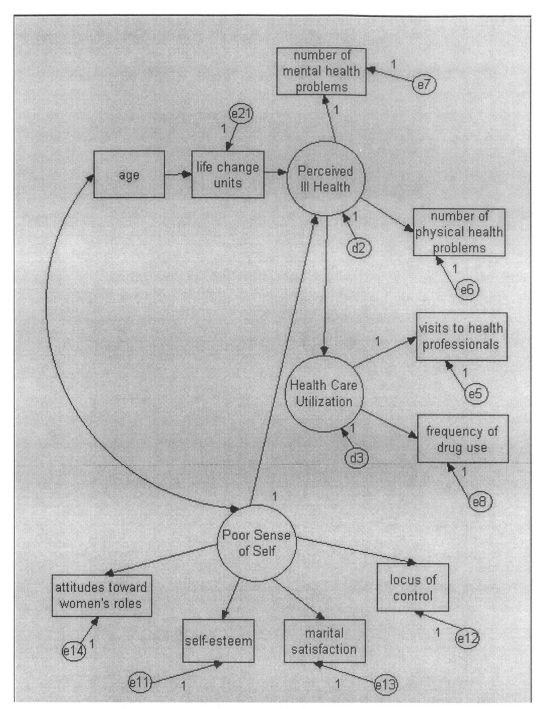

Figure 14.15   **Analysis Properties** dialog box for SEM of health variables.

Note that a request has been made for tests for normality and outliers. Using procedures described in Section 14.2.3, the SEM model is estimated, producing *Output 14.2.*

Your model contains the following variables

attrole	observed	endogenous
control	observed	endogenous
esteem	observed	endogenous
attmar	observed	endogenous
phyheal	observed	endogenous
timedrs	observed	endogenous
druguse	observed	endogenous
scstress	observed	endogenous
menheal	observed	endogenous
age	observed	exogenous
Perceived_Ill Health	unobserved	endogenous
Health Care_Utilization	unobserved	endogenous
Poor Sense_of Self	unobserved	exogenous
e11	unobserved	exogenous
d2	unobserved	exogenous
d3	unobserved	exogenous
e21	unobserved	exogenous
e6	unobserved	exogenous
e5	unobserved	exogenous
e8	unobserved	exogenous
e13	unobserved	exogenous
e14	unobserved	exogenous
e12	unobserved	exogenous
e7	unobserved	exogenous

Number of variables in your model:	24
Number of observed variables:	10
Number of unobserved variables:	14
Number of exogenous variables:	13
Number of endogenous variables:	11

Summary of Parameters

	Weights	Covariances	Variances	Means	Intercepts	Total
Fixed	13	0	1	0	0	14
Labeled	0	0	0	0	0	0
Unlabeled	10	1	12	0	0	23
Total	23	1	13	0	0	37

The model is recursive.

Sample size = 445

Computation of degrees of freedom

    Number of distinct sample moments = 55
    Number of distinct parameters to be estimated = 23
    Degrees of freedom = 55 - 23 = 32

Minimum was achieved

Chi-square = 162.703
Degrees of freedom = 32
Probability level = 0.000

Assessment of normality

	min	max	skew	c.r.	kurtosis	c.r.
age	0.000	8.000	0.032	0.278	-1.176	-5.064
scstress	0.000	6.430	0.767	6.607	0.224	0.965
menheal	0.000	18.000	0.600	5.168	-0.297	-1.277
druguse	0.000	42.000	1.261	10.862	1.033	4.448
timedrs	0.000	60.000	2.875	24.758	9.719	41.848
phyheal	2.000	14.000	0.963	8.295	0.788	3.392
attmar	0.000	58.000	0.776	6.683	0.835	3.595
esteem	8.000	29.000	0.506	4.355	0.304	1.310
control	5.000	10.000	0.509	4.382	-0.377	-1.624
attrole	18.000	55.000	0.045	0.384	-0.410	-1.763
Multivariate					23.407	15.936

Observations farthest from the centroid (Mahalanobis distance)

Observation number	Mahalanobis d-squared	p1	p2
164	43.609	0.000	0.002
268	41.503	0.000	0.000
39	39.335	0.000	0.000
200	38.944	0.000	0.000
265	37.713	0.000	0.000
240	36.895	0.000	0.000
160	35.977	0.000	0.000
352	32.306	0.000	0.000
188	32.230	0.000	0.000
372	32.204	0.000	0.000
356	31.495	0.000	0.000
111	31.365	0.001	0.000
374	31.079	0.001	0.000
295	27.350	0.002	0.000
205	27.231	0.002	0.000
83	25.435	0.005	0.000
210	25.222	0.005	0.000
238	24.949	0.005	0.000
364	23.368	0.009	0.000
274	23.249	0.010	0.000

Regression Weights

			Estimate	S.E.	C.R.	P	Label
scstress	<−	age	-0.170	0.027	-6.398	0.000	
Perceived_Ill Health	<−	Poor Sense_of Self	0.788	0.185	4.270	0.000	
Perceived_Ill Health	<−	scstress	1.119	0.124	9.006	0.000	
Health Care_Utilization	<−	Perceived_Ill Health	1.763	0.206	8.571	0.000	
attrole	<−	Poor Sense_of Self	1.186	0.395	3.003	0.003	
control	<−	Poor Sense_of Self	0.579	0.081	7.151	0.000	
esteem	<−	Poor Sense_of Self	3.067	0.330	9.291	0.000	
attmar	<−	Poor Sense_of Self	3.429	0.544	6.307	0.000	
phyheal	<−	Perceived_Ill Health	0.598	0.053	11.216	0.000	
timedrs	<−	Health Care_Utilization	1.000				
druguse	<−	Health Care_Utilization	0.976	0.123	7.910	0.000	
menheal	<−	Perceived_Ill Health	1.000				

Standardized Regression Weights

			Estimate
scstress	<−	age	-0.291
Perceived_Ill Health	<−	Poor Sense_of Self	0.270
Perceived_Ill Health	<−	scstress	0.501
Health Care_Utilization	<−	Perceived_Ill Health	0.975
attrole	<−	Poor Sense_of Self	0.175
control	<−	Poor Sense_of Self	0.457
esteem	<−	Poor Sense_of Self	0.774
attmar	<−	Poor Sense_of Self	0.385
phyheal	<−	Perceived_Ill Health	0.739
timedrs	<−	Health Care_Utilization	0.521
druguse	<−	Health Care_Utilization	0.562
menheal	<−	Perceived_Ill Health	0.691

Covariances

			Estimate	S.E.	C.R.	P	Label
Poor Sense_of Self	<−>	age	-0.028	0.129	-0.220	0.826	

200

Correlations

	Estimate
Poor Sense_of Self <-> age	-0.013

Variances

	Estimate	S.E.	C.R.	P	Label
Poor Sense_of Self	1.000				
age	4.943	0.332	14.900	0.000	
e21	1.558	0.105	14.900	0.000	
d2	5.735	0.872	6.574	0.000	
d3	1.368	3.821	0.358	0.720	
e11	6.303	1.830	3.445	0.001	
e6	2.518	0.276	9.118	0.000	
e5	74.422	6.241	11.925	0.000	
e8	57.312	5.243	10.930	0.000	
e13	67.663	5.170	13.087	0.000	
e14	44.482	3.036	14.650	0.000	
e12	1.270	0.108	11.744	0.000	
e7	9.297	0.887	10.487	0.000	

Squared Multiple Correlations

	Estimate
scstress	0.084
Perceived_Ill Health	0.325
Health Care_Utilization	0.951
menheal	0.477
druguse	0.316
timedrs	0.272
phyheal	0.547
attmar	0.148
esteem	0.599
control	0.209
attrole	0.031

Residual Covariances

	age	scstress	menheal	druguse	timedrs	phyheal	attmar	esteem	control	attrole
age	0.000	0.000	0.114	0.947	1.210	0.657	-1.854	0.233	-0.367	3.306
scstress	0.000	0.000	0.205	0.369	0.035	-0.220	1.270	-0.539	0.104	-2.126
menheal	0.114	0.205	-0.124	-0.533	-4.186	-0.157	6.298	1.269	1.061	-3.037
druguse	0.947	0.369	-0.533	-0.366	-0.375	0.142	2.168	-5.989	0.018	-7.653
timedrs	1.210	0.035	-4.186	-0.375	-0.384	1.906	-0.555	-3.644	-0.508	-7.218
phyheal	0.657	-0.220	-0.157	0.142	1.906	-0.044	0.038	-0.721	0.066	-1.356
attmar	-1.854	1.270	6.298	2.168	-0.555	0.038	0.000	0.009	0.299	-8.213
esteem	0.233	-0.539	1.269	-5.989	-3.644	-0.721	0.009	0.000	-0.043	1.630
control	-0.367	0.104	1.061	0.018	-0.508	0.066	0.299	-0.043	0.000	-0.652
attrole	3.306	-2.126	-3.037	-7.653	-7.218	-1.356	-8.213	1.630	-0.652	0.000

Standardized Residual Covariances

	age	scstress	menheal	druguse	timedrs	phyheal	attmar	esteem	control	attrole
age	0.000	0.000	0.255	0.977	1.131	2.627	-1.971	0.557	-2.748	4.625
scstress	0.000	0.000	0.743	0.629	0.055	-1.415	2.302	-2.198	1.330	-5.070
menheal	0.255	0.743	-0.103	-0.272	-1.952	-0.297	3.521	1.582	4.169	-2.238
druguse	0.977	0.629	-0.272	-0.065	-0.082	0.128	0.559	-3.456	0.033	-2.600
timedrs	1.131	0.055	-1.952	-0.082	-0.056	1.578	-0.130	-1.906	-0.834	-2.220
phyheal	2.627	-1.415	-0.297	0.128	1.578	-0.118	0.038	-1.607	0.462	-1.789
attmar	-1.971	2.302	3.521	0.559	-0.130	0.038	0.000	0.005	0.549	-2.860
esteem	0.557	-2.198	1.582	-3.456	-1.906	-1.607	0.005	0.000	-0.171	1.267
control	-2.748	1.330	4.169	0.033	-0.834	0.462	0.549	-0.171	0.000	-1.597
attrole	4.625	-5.070	-2.238	-2.600	-2.220	-1.789	-2.860	1.267	-1.597	0.000

Modification Indices

Covariances:

			M.I.	Par Change
d2	<–>	age	4.585	0.674
d3	<–>	Poor Sense_of Self	13.435	-1.377
e7	<–>	Poor Sense_of Self	22.268	0.939
e7	<–>	d2	6.776	-1.189
e7	<–>	d3	7.685	-2.850
e8	<–>	Poor Sense_of Self	9.258	-1.419
e5	<–>	e7	13.302	-5.327
e6	<–>	age	7.758	0.549
e6	<–>	d3	8.949	1.654
e6	<–>	e5	13.982	2.959
e13	<–>	age	4.840	-1.966
e13	<–>	e21	6.370	1.266
e13	<–>	e7	6.785	3.597
e11	<–>	e21	7.230	-0.561
e11	<–>	d3	8.520	-3.162
e11	<–>	e7	4.911	1.271
e11	<–>	e8	10.257	-4.308
e12	<–>	age	10.453	-0.402
e12	<–>	e7	13.163	0.697
e14	<–>	age	22.303	3.341
e14	<–>	e21	14.177	-1.495
e14	<–>	e13	10.660	-8.798
e14	<–>	e11	8.281	3.209

Variances: M.I.   Par Change

Regression Weights:			M.I.	Par Change
Perceived_Ill Health	<--	age	4.584	0.136
Health Care_Utilization	<--	Poor Sense_of Self	13.495	-1.380
menheal	<--	Poor Sense_of Self	22.428	0.942
menheal	<--	timedrs	9.338	-0.049
menheal	<--	attmar	14.651	0.070
menheal	<--	esteem	16.038	0.165
menheal	<--	control	23.589	0.625
druguse	<--	Poor Sense_of Self	9.280	-1.421
druguse	<--	esteem	11.405	-0.326
timedrs	<--	menheal	5.601	-0.241
timedrs	<--	phyheal	4.715	0.396
phyheal	<--	age	7.825	0.112
phyheal	<--	scstress	5.043	-0.153
phyheal	<--	timedrs	9.934	0.028
attmar	<--	age	4.839	-0.398
attmar	<--	scstress	9.327	0.941
attmar	<--	Perceived_Ill Health	5.091	0.355
attmar	<--	Health Care_Utilization	4.984	0.197
attmar	<--	menheal	9.230	0.290
attmar	<--	attrole	10.232	-0.190
esteem	<--	scstress	8.593	-0.376
esteem	<--	Perceived_Ill Health	5.947	-0.159
esteem	<--	Health Care_Utilization	6.465	-0.093
esteem	<--	druguse	13.923	-0.068
esteem	<--	attrole	8.025	0.070
control	<--	age	10.451	-0.081
control	<--	scstress	4.718	0.093
control	<--	Perceived_Ill Health	5.862	0.053
control	<--	Health Care_Utilization	5.511	0.029
control	<--	menheal	14.401	0.050
attrole	<--	age	22.299	0.676
attrole	<--	scstress	24.748	-1.214
attrole	<--	Perceived_Ill Health	11.499	-0.422
attrole	<--	Health Care_Utilization	11.519	-0.237
attrole	<--	menheal	7.084	-0.201
attrole	<--	druguse	5.023	-0.078

Fit Measures

Fit Measure	Default model	Saturated	Independence	Macro
Discrepancy	162.703	0.000	744.591	CMIN
Degrees of freedom	32	0	45	DF
P	0.000		0.000	P
Number of parameters	23	55	10	NPAR
Discrepancy / df	5.084		16.546	CMINDF
RMR	2.470	0.000	5.577	RMR
GFI	0.928	1.000	0.703	GFI
Adjusted GFI	0.875		0.637	AGFI
Parsimony-adjusted GFI	0.540		0.575	PGFI
Normed fit index	0.781	1.000	0.000	NFI
Relative fit index	0.693		0.000	RFI
Incremental fit index	0.817	1.000	0.000	IFI
Tucker-Lewis index	0.737		0.000	TLI
Comparative fit index	0.813	1.000	0.000	CFI
Parsimony ratio	0.711	0.000	1.000	PRATIO
Parsimony-adjusted NFI	0.556	0.000	0.000	PNFI
Parsimony-adjusted CFI	0.578	0.000	0.000	PCFI
Noncentrality parameter estimate	130.703	0.000	699.591	NCP
NCP lower bound	94.557	0.000	614.865	NCPLO
NCP upper bound	174.377	0.000	791.742	NCPHI
FMIN	0.366	0.000	1.677	FMIN
F0	0.294	0.000	1.576	F0
F0 lower bound	0.213	0.000	1.385	F0LO
F0 upper bound	0.393	0.000	1.783	F0HI
RMSEA	0.096		0.187	RMSEA
RMSEA lower bound	0.082		0.175	RMSEALO
RMSEA upper bound	0.111		0.199	RMSEAHI
P for test of close fit	0.000		0.000	PCLOSE
Akaike information criterion (AIC)	208.703	110.000	764.591	AIC
Browne-Cudeck criterion	209.872	112.794	765.099	BCC
Bayes information criterion	355.918	462.036	828.597	BIC
Consistent AIC	325.959	390.394	815.571	CAIC
Expected cross validation index	0.470	0.248	1.722	ECVI
ECVI lower bound	0.389	0.248	1.531	ECVILO
ECVI upper bound	0.568	0.248	1.930	ECVIHI
MECVI	0.473	0.254	1.723	MECVI
Hoelter .05 index	127		37	HFIVE
Hoelter .01 index	146		42	HONE

Fit Measures

	CMIN	DF	P	NPAR	CMINDF	RMR	GFI	AGFI	PGFI
Default model	162.703	32	0.000	23	5.084	2.470	0.928	0.875	0.540
Saturated	0.000	0		55		0.000	1.000		
Independence	744.591	45	0.000	10	16.546	5.577	0.703	0.637	0.575

14.4.2 SEM Model Modification

The model fit differs a bit from that in *UMS* because of the difference in estimation techniques (lack of robust estimation here). The suggestion of a path between Poor Sense of Self and MENHEAL shows up in the **Modification Indices** tables **labeled Regression Weights** and **Covariances** (where e7 is error for MENHEAL. Figure 14.16 shows the addition of the path.

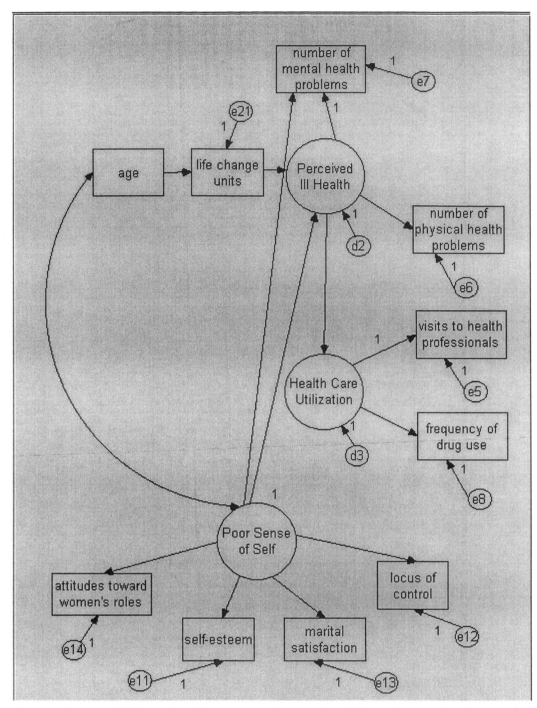

Figure 14.16   Addition of path between MENHEAL and Poor Sense of Self.

Output 14.3 shows some of the fit information from the model with the added path.

Output 14.3 **GOODNESS OF FIT INFORMATION AFTER ADDITION OF MENTAL HEALTH PREDICTED BY POOR SENSE OF SELF.**

Fit Measures

Fit Measure	Default model	Saturated	Independence	Macro
Discrepancy	127.550	0.000	744.591	CMIN
Degrees of freedom	31	0	45	DF
P	0.000		0.000	P
Number of parameters	24	55	10	NPAR
Discrepancy / df	4.115		16.546	CMINDF
RMR	2.038	0.000	5.577	RMR
GFI	0.942	1.000	0.703	GFI
Adjusted GFI	0.898		0.637	AGFI
Parsimony-adjusted GFI	0.531		0.575	PGFI
Normed fit index	0.829	1.000	0.000	NFI
Relative fit index	0.751		0.000	RFI
Incremental fit index	0.865	1.000	0.000	IFI
Tucker-Lewis index	0.800		0.000	TLI
Comparative fit index	0.862	1.000	0.000	CFI
Parsimony ratio	0.689	0.000	1.000	PRATIO
Parsimony-adjusted NFI	0.571	0.000	0.000	PNFI
Parsimony-adjusted CFI	0.594	0.000	0.000	PCFI

Noncentrality parameter estimate	96.550	0.000	699.591	NCP
NCP lower bound	65.436	0.000	614.865	NCPLO
NCP upper bound	135.226	0.000	791.742	NCPHI
FMIN	0.287	0.000	1.677	FMIN
F0	0.217	0.000	1.576	F0
F0 lower bound	0.147	0.000	1.385	F0LO
F0 upper bound	0.305	0.000	1.783	F0HI
RMSEA	0.084		0.187	RMSEA
RMSEA lower bound	0.069		0.175	RMSEALO
RMSEA upper bound	0.099		0.199	RMSEAHI
P for test of close fit	0.000		0.000	PCLOSE
Akaike information criterion (AIC)	175.550	110.000	764.591	AIC
Browne-Cudeck criterion	176.769	112.794	765.099	BCC
Bayes information criterion	329.166	462.036	828.597	BIC
Consistent AIC	297.904	390.394	815.571	CAIC
Expected cross validation index	0.395	0.248	1.722	ECVI
ECVI lower bound	0.325	0.248	1.531	ECVILO
ECVI upper bound	0.482	0.248	1.930	ECVIHI
MECVI	0.398	0.254	1.723	MECVI
Hoelter .05 index	157		37	HFIVE
Hoelter .01 index	182		42	HONE

Fit Measures

	CMIN	DF	P	NPAR	CMINDF	RMR	GFI	AGFI	PGFI
Default model	127.550	31	0.000	24	4.115	2.038	0.942	0.898	0.531
Saturated	0.000	0		55		0.000	1.000		
Independence	744.591	45	0.000	10	16.546	5.577	0.703	0.637	0.575

Figure 14.17 shows the final model as specified.

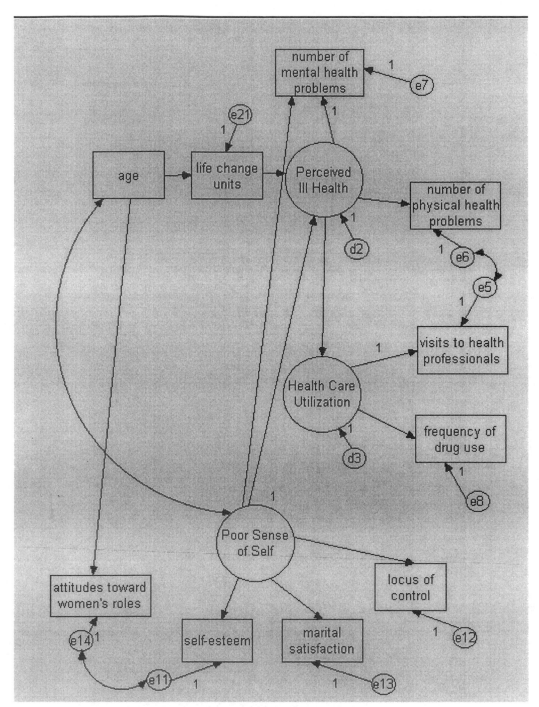

Figure 14.17   Setup for final SEM model.

Figure 14.18 shows the output selections for the final model.

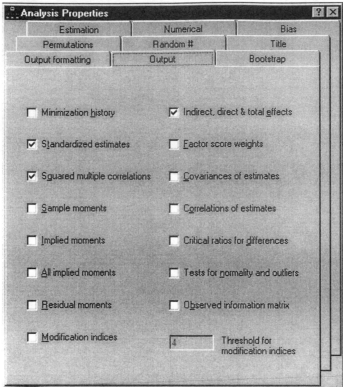

Figure 14.18   Selection of Analysis Properties for final
SEM Model.

Output 14.4 shows the results of running the final SEM model.

Output 14.4 **EDITED OUTPUT FOR FINAL SEM MODEL.**

Your model contains the following variables

control	observed	endogenous
esteem	observed	endogenous
attmar	observed	endogenous
phyheal	observed	endogenous
timedrs	observed	endogenous
druguse	observed	endogenous
scstress	observed	endogenous
attrole	observed	endogenous
menheal	observed	endogenous
age	observed	exogenous
Perceived_Ill Health	unobserved	endogenous
Health Care_Utilization	unobserved	endogenous
Poor Sense_of Self	unobserved	exogenous
e11	unobserved	exogenous
d2	unobserved	exogenous
d3	unobserved	exogenous
e21	unobserved	exogenous
e8	unobserved	exogenous
e13	unobserved	exogenous
e14	unobserved	exogenous
e12	unobserved	exogenous
e7	unobserved	exogenous
e5	unobserved	exogenous
e6	unobserved	exogenous

Number of variables in your model:	24
Number of observed variables:	10
Number of unobserved variables:	14
Number of exogenous variables:	13
Number of endogenous variables:	11

Summary of Parameters

	Weights	Covariances	Variances	Means	Intercepts	Total
Fixed	13	0	1	0	0	14
Labeled	0	0	0	0	0	0
Unlabeled	11	3	12	0	0	26
Total	24	3	13	0	0	40

The model is recursive.

Sample size = 445

Computation of degrees of freedom

Number of distinct sample moments = 55
Number of distinct parameters to be estimated = 26
Degrees of freedom = 55 - 26 = 29

Minimum was achieved

Chi-square = 69.064
Degrees of freedom = 29
Probability level = 0.000

Regression Weights

			Estimate	S.E.	C.R.	P	Label
scstress	<−	age	-0.170	0.027	-6.398	0.000	
Perceived_Ill Health	<−	Poor Sense_of Self	0.410	0.210	1.954	0.051	
Perceived_Ill Health	<−	scstress	1.100	0.125	8.798	0.000	
Health Care_Utilization	<−	Perceived_Ill Health	1.452	0.236	6.139	0.000	
control	<−	Poor Sense_of Self	0.689	0.076	9.015	0.000	
esteem	<−	Poor Sense_of Self	2.456	0.243	10.109	0.000	
attmar	<−	Poor Sense_of Self	4.076	0.529	7.710	0.000	
phyheal	<−	Perceived_Ill Health	0.573	0.060	9.593	0.000	
timedrs	<−	Health Care_Utilization	1.000				
druguse	<−	Health Care_Utilization	1.275	0.205	6.230	0.000	
menheal	<−	Perceived_Ill Health	1.000				
menheal	<−	Poor Sense_of Self	1.394	0.234	5.950	0.000	
attrole	<−	age	0.588	0.139	4.242	0.000	

Standardized Regression Weights

			Estimate
scstress	<−	age	-0.291
Perceived_Ill Health	<−	Poor Sense_of Self	0.148
Perceived_Ill Health	<−	scstress	0.517
Health Care_Utilization	<−	Perceived_Ill Health	0.898
control	<−	Poor Sense_of Self	0.544
esteem	<−	Poor Sense_of Self	0.620
attmar	<−	Poor Sense_of Self	0.457
phyheal	<−	Perceived_Ill Health	0.677
timedrs	<−	Health Care_Utilization	0.445
druguse	<−	Health Care_Utilization	0.627
menheal	<−	Perceived_Ill Health	0.661
menheal	<−	Poor Sense_of Self	0.332
attrole	<−	age	0.194

Covariances

			Estimate	S.E.	C.R.	P	Label
Poor Sense_of Self	<−>	age	-0.220	0.135	-1.632	0.103	
e11	<−>	e14	5.190	1.147	4.526	0.000	
e5	<−>	e6	4.386	1.055	4.157	0.000	

Correlations

	Estimate
Poor Sense_of Self <—> age	-0.099
e11 <—> e14	0.252
e5 <—> e6	0.281

Variances

	Estimate	S.E.	C.R.	P	Label
Poor Sense_of Self	1.000				
age	4.943	0.332	14.900	0.000	
e21	1.558	0.105	14.900	0.000	
d2	5.442	0.900	6.050	0.000	
d3	3.893	2.830	1.376	0.169	
e11	9.681	1.098	8.817	0.000	
e8	50.623	6.396	7.915	0.000	
e13	62.802	5.070	12.387	0.000	
e14	43.750	2.936	14.900	0.000	
e12	1.130	0.105	10.777	0.000	
e7	6.701	0.898	7.463	0.000	
e5	81.482	6.378	12.776	0.000	
e6	2.980	0.300	9.933	0.000	

Squared Multiple Correlations

	Estimate
scstress	0.084
Perceived_Ill Health	0.293
Health Care_Utilization	0.807
menheal	0.619
attrole	0.038
druguse	0.393
timedrs	0.198
phyheal	0.459
attmar	0.209
esteem	0.384
control	0.296

Total Effects - Estimates

	age	Poor Sense_of Self	scstress	Perceived_Ill Health	Health Care_Utilization
scstress	-0.170	0.000	0.000	0.000	0.000
Perceived_Ill Health	-0.187	0.410	1.100	0.000	0.000
Health Care_Utilization	-0.272	0.595	1.597	1.452	0.000
menheal	-0.187	1.804	1.100	1.000	0.000
attrole	0.588	0.000	0.000	0.000	0.000
druguse	-0.347	0.759	2.036	1.851	1.275
timedrs	-0.272	0.595	1.597	1.452	1.000
phyheal	-0.107	0.235	0.630	0.573	0.000
attmar	0.000	4.076	0.000	0.000	0.000
esteem	0.000	2.456	0.000	0.000	0.000
control	0.000	0.689	0.000	0.000	0.000

Standardized Total Effects - Estimates

	age	Poor Sense_of Self	scstress	Perceived_Ill Health	Health Care_Utilization
scstress	-0.291	0.000	0.000	0.000	0.000
Perceived_Ill Health	-0.150	0.148	0.517	0.000	0.000
Health Care_Utilization	-0.135	0.133	0.464	0.898	0.000
menheal	-0.099	0.430	0.342	0.661	0.000
attrole	0.194	0.000	0.000	0.000	0.000
druguse	-0.085	0.083	0.291	0.563	0.627
timedrs	-0.060	0.059	0.207	0.400	0.445
phyheal	-0.102	0.100	0.350	0.677	0.000
attmar	0.000	0.457	0.000	0.000	0.000
esteem	0.000	0.620	0.000	0.000	0.000
control	0.000	0.544	0.000	0.000	0.000

Direct Effects - Estimates

	age	Poor Sense_of Self	scstress	Perceived_Ill Health	Health Care_Utilization
scstress	-0.170	0.000	0.000	0.000	0.000
Perceived_Ill Health	0.000	0.410	1.100	0.000	0.000
Health Care_Utilization	0.000	0.000	0.000	1.452	0.000
menheal	0.000	1.394	0.000	1.000	0.000
attrole	0.588	0.000	0.000	0.000	0.000
druguse	0.000	0.000	0.000	0.000	1.275
timedrs	0.000	0.000	0.000	0.000	1.000
phyheal	0.000	0.000	0.000	0.573	0.000
attmar	0.000	4.076	0.000	0.000	0.000
esteem	0.000	2.456	0.000	0.000	0.000
control	0.000	0.689	0.000	0.000	0.000

Standardized Direct Effects - Estimates

	age	Poor Sense_of Self	scstress	Perceived_III Health	Health Care_Utilization
scstress	-0.291	0.000	0.000	0.000	0.000
Perceived_III Health	0.000	0.148	0.517	0.000	0.000
Health Care_Utilization	0.000	0.000	0.000	0.898	0.000
menheal	0.000	0.332	0.000	0.661	0.000
attrole	0.194	0.000	0.000	0.000	0.000
druguse	0.000	0.000	0.000	0.000	0.627
timedrs	0.000	0.000	0.000	0.000	0.445
phyheal	0.000	0.000	0.000	0.677	0.000
attmar	0.000	0.457	0.000	0.000	0.000
esteem	0.000	0.620	0.000	0.000	0.000
control	0.000	0.544	0.000	0.000	0.000

Indirect Effects - Estimates

	age	Poor Sense_of Self	scstress	Perceived_III Health	Health Care_Utilization
scstress	0.000	0.000	0.000	0.000	0.000
Perceived_III Health	-0.187	0.000	0.000	0.000	0.000
Health Care_Utilization	-0.272	0.595	1.597	0.000	0.000
menheal	-0.187	0.410	1.100	0.000	0.000
attrole	0.000	0.000	0.000	0.000	0.000
druguse	-0.347	0.759	2.036	1.851	0.000
timedrs	-0.272	0.595	1.597	1.452	0.000
phyheal	-0.107	0.235	0.630	0.000	0.000
attmar	0.000	0.000	0.000	0.000	0.000
esteem	0.000	0.000	0.000	0.000	0.000
control	0.000	0.000	0.000	0.000	0.000

Standardized Indirect Effects - Estimates

	age	Poor Sense_of Self	scstress	Perceived_III Health	Health Care_Utilization
scstress	0.000	0.000	0.000	0.000	0.000
Perceived_III Health	-0.150	0.000	0.000	0.000	0.000
Health Care_Utilization	-0.135	0.133	0.464	0.000	0.000
menheal	-0.099	0.098	0.342	0.000	0.000
attrole	0.000	0.000	0.000	0.000	0.000
druguse	-0.085	0.083	0.291	0.563	0.000
timedrs	-0.060	0.059	0.207	0.400	0.000
phyheal	-0.102	0.100	0.350	0.000	0.000
attmar	0.000	0.000	0.000	0.000	0.000
esteem	0.000	0.000	0.000	0.000	0.000
control	0.000	0.000	0.000	0.000	0.000

Fit Measures

Fit Measure	Default model	Saturated	Independence	Macro
Discrepancy	69.064	0.000	744.591	CMIN
Degrees of freedom	29	0	45	DF
P	0.000		0.000	P
Number of parameters	26	55	10	NPAR
Discrepancy / df	2.382		16.546	CMINDF
RMR	1.418	0.000	5.577	RMR
GFI	0.970	1.000	0.703	GFI
Adjusted GFI	0.944		0.637	AGFI
Parsimony-adjusted GFI	0.512		0.575	PGFI
Normed fit index	0.907	1.000	0.000	NFI
Relative fit index	0.856		0.000	RFI
Incremental fit index	0.944	1.000	0.000	IFI
Tucker-Lewis index	0.911		0.000	TLI
Comparative fit index	0.943	1.000	0.000	CFI
Parsimony ratio	0.644	0.000	1.000	PRATIO
Parsimony-adjusted NFI	0.585	0.000	0.000	PNFI
Parsimony-adjusted CFI	0.608	0.000	0.000	PCFI
Noncentrality parameter estimate	40.064	0.000	699.591	NCP
NCP lower bound	19.520	0.000	614.865	NCPLO
NCP upper bound	68.311	0.000	791.742	NCPHI
FMIN	0.156	0.000	1.677	FMIN
F0	0.090	0.000	1.576	F0
F0 lower bound	0.044	0.000	1.385	F0LO
F0 upper bound	0.154	0.000	1.783	F0HI
RMSEA	0.056		0.187	RMSEA
RMSEA lower bound	0.039		0.175	RMSEALO
RMSEA upper bound	0.073		0.199	RMSEAHI
P for test of close fit	0.268		0.000	PCLOSE
Akaike information criterion (AIC)	121.064	110.000	764.591	AIC
Browne-Cudeck criterion	122.385	112.794	765.099	BCC
Bayes information criterion	287.482	462.036	828.597	BIC
Consistent AIC	253.614	390.394	815.571	CAIC
Expected cross validation index	0.273	0.248	1.722	ECVI
ECVI lower bound	0.226	0.248	1.531	ECVILO
ECVI upper bound	0.336	0.248	1.930	ECVIHI
MECVI	0.276	0.254	1.723	MECVI
Hoelter .05 index	274		37	HFIVE
Hoelter .01 index	319		42	HONE

Fit Measures

	CMIN	DF	P	NPAR	CMINDF	RMR	GFI	AGFI	PGFI
Default model	69.064	29	0.000	26	2.382	1.418	0.970	0.944	0.512
Saturated	0.000	0		55		0.000	1.000		
Independence	744.591	45	0.000	10	16.546	5.577	0.703	0.637	0.575

Figure 14.19 shows the full model with standardized coefficients as produced by AMOS. Diagram is accessed as shown in Section 14.2.4.

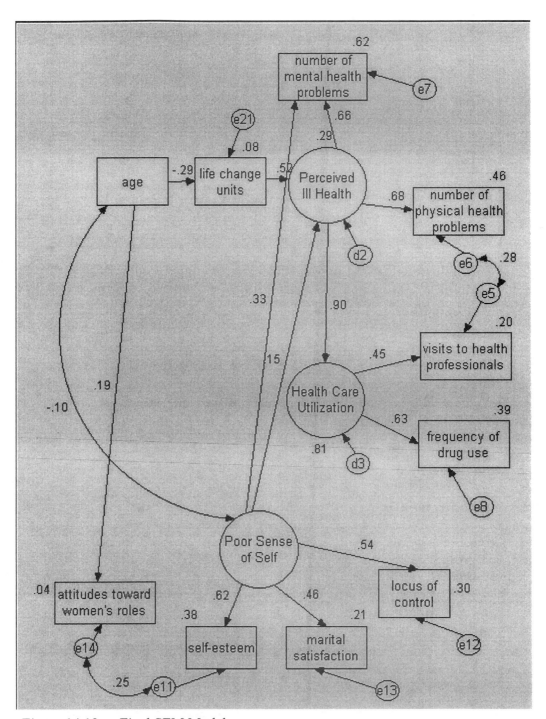

Figure 14.19   Final SEM Model

Chapter 15. Survival/Failure Analysis

This chapter demonstrates survival analysis using SPSS for Windows, for the complete example of Chapter 15 in *Using Multivariate Statistics*. The file to use is SURVIVAL.sav on the Internet site. (See Section 3.1 of Chapter 3 for detailed information on obtaining the SPSS files.)

Differences in survival time following treatment with either an experimental drug or a placebo are examined in the 312 subjects who participated in the trial. Additional covariates are age (in days), serum bilirubin in mg/dl, serum albumin in gm/dl, prothrombin time in seconds, and presence of edema. Edema has three levels treated as continuous: 1) no edema and no diuretic therapy for edema, coded as "0.00"; 2) edema present without diuretics or edema resolved by diuretics, coded "0.50"; and 3) edema despite diuretic therapy, coded "1.00." Coding for status is 0 = censored, 1 = liver transplant, and 2 = event.

15.1   EVALUATION OF ASSUMPTIONS

The preliminary run for descriptives and saving standard scores for each covariate is done by choosing the following SPSS commands, and as shown in Figures 15.1 and 15.2.

>Analyze
>Descriptive Statistics
>Descriptives...
    Variable(s)
        • age
        • albumin
        • bilirubi
        • drug
        • edema
        • prothom
    ☑Save standardized values as variables
    Options...
        ☑Mean
    Dispersion
        ☑Std. Deviation
        ☑Minimum
        ☑Maximum
    Distribution
        ☑Kurtosis
        ☑Skewness

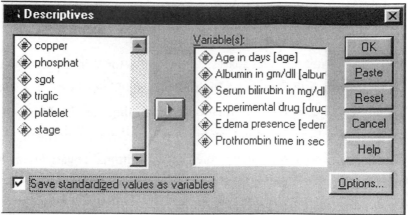

Figure 15.1 **Descriptives** dialog box with Survival variables entered.

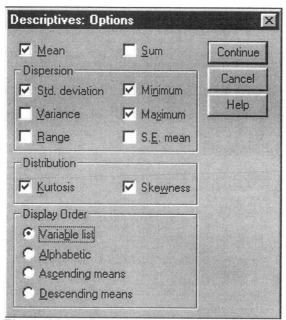

Figure 15.2   **Descriptives: Options** dialog
box with options selected.

Table 15.15 of *UMS* is produced as output, and *z* scores are added to the data file.

Figure 15.3 shows the procedure for finding minimum and maximum *z* scores through the
Descriptives dialog box. Previous variables are de-selected and the six new *z* score variables are added to
the **Variable(s):** list. **Options...** other than minimum and maximum are de-selected in the **Options** dialog
box (not shown).

222

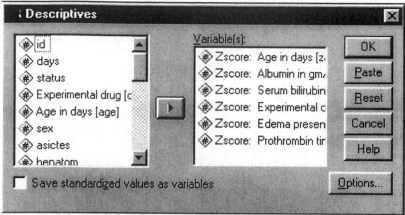

Figure 15.3   **Descriptives** dialog box with z score for Survival
variables entered.

The output for these procedures is shown in Table 15.16 of *UMS*.

Logarithmic transformation of BILIRUB is done as per Section 4.1.5 of this workbook.
Transformation of AGE is done through by following these SPSS commands and as shown in Figure
15.4.

```
>Transform
      >Compute...
            Target Variable:   y_age
            Numeric Expression:    age/365.25
```

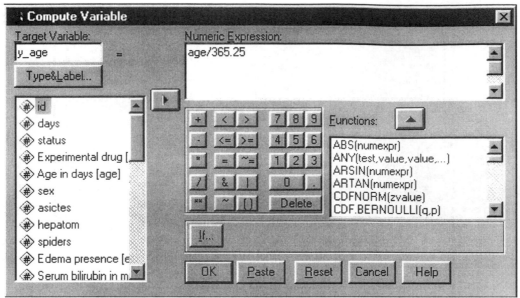

Figure 15.4 **Compute Variable** dialog box with computed variable shown.

Table 15.17 of *UMS* is produced by repeating Figures 15.1 and 15.2 with LBILIRUB and Y_AGE chosen as **Variable(s):**. Mahalanobis distance is found through regression by selecting these SPSS commands.

>Analyze
   >Regression
      >Linear...
         Dependent:
            • id
         Independent(s):
            • albumin
            • drug
            • edema
            • prothom
            • lbilirub
            • y_age
      >Save...
         Distances
            ☑Mahalanobis

Mahalanobis distances are added to the data file in a column labeled mah_1. These distance values can be viewed individually, or may be viewed by selecting cases on the basis of the criterion and summarizing those cases in a table that shows all of the covariates, Mahalanobis distance, and the case identification number.

Case selection follows the procedures of Section 4.1.2, with the condition to be satisfied filled in as mah_1 > 22.458. As seen in Figure 15.5, summarization is accomplished by choosing the following SPSS commands.

>Analyze
  >Reports
    >Case Summaries...
      Variables:
        • albumin
        • drug
        • edema
        • prothom
        • bilirub
        • y_age

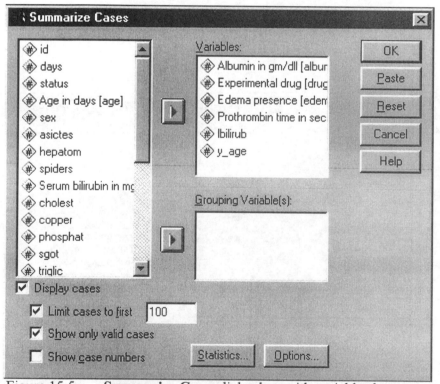

Figure 15.5   **Summarize Cases** dialog box with variable shown.

This results in Table 15.18 of *UMS*. Identification of covariates causing multivariate outliers is done through regression as per Section 4.1.7. The three multivariate outliers are omitted from subsequent analyses by selection procedures of Section 4.1.2, with the condition to be satisfied filled in as mah_1 <= 22.458.

Differences between liver transplant and other censored cases are found through regression after forming a dummy variable based on whether there was a liver transplant. The dummy variable, XPLANT, is formed in two transformations. First, XPLANT is declared to be a new variable with all values = 0. Then, the value of XPLANT is changed to one for those whose status = 1 (i.e., liver transplant patients).

>Transform
>Compute
Target Variable: xplant
Numeric Expression: = 0

Figure 15.6 shows the **Compute Variable** dialog box for creating XPLANT and assigned a value of "0" to all cases.

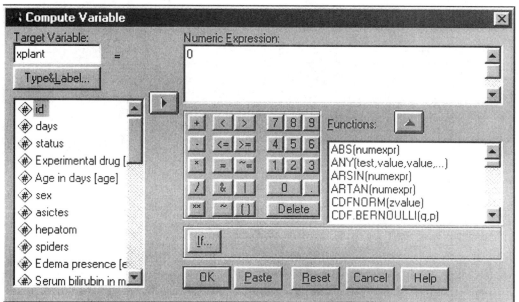

Figure 15.6   **Compute Variable** dialog box with Target variable and Numeric Expression shown.

Figures 15.7 and 15.8 show SPSS dialog boxes for the second transformation, in which liver transplant patients are coded "1" for XPLANT. For this operation, make the following SPSS choices.

>Transform
　>Compute
　　Target Variable: xplant
　　Numeric Expression: = 1
　　If...
　⊙Include if case satisfies condition
　　status = 1

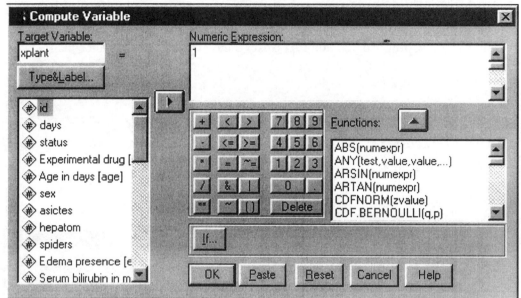

Figure 15.7   **Compute Variable** dialog box with new Target variable and Numeric Expression shown.

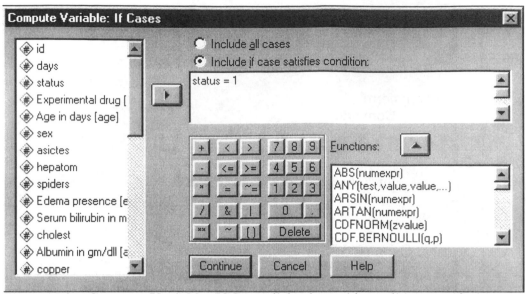

Figure 15.8   **Compute Variable: If Cases** dialog box with condition specified.

Standard multiple regression then is run using XPLANT as the DV and the six covariates as IVs (ALBUMIN, DRUG, EDEMA, LBILIRUB, PROTHOM, Y_AGE), as per Figure 15.9. This produces Table 15.20 of *UMS* as output.

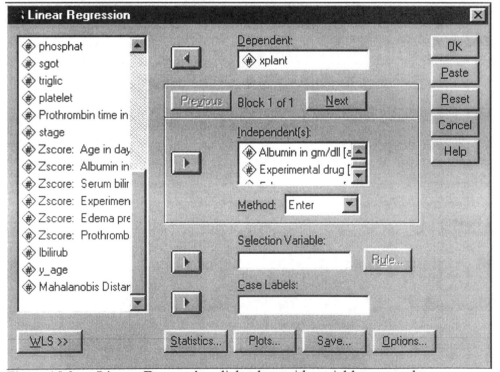

Figure 15.9   **Linear Regression** dialog box with variables entered.

Proportionality of hazards is tested by choosing the following SPSS commands.

>Analyze
>Survival
>Cox w/Time-Dep Cov...
Expression for T_COV_ : LN(T_)
Model...
Time:
• days
Status:
• status
Define event...
Value(s) Indicating Event Has Occurred:
⊙ Single value: 2
Covariates:
• albumin
• drug
• edema
• prothom
• lbilirub
• y_age
• T_COV_*albumin
• T_COV_*drug
• T_COV_*edema
• T_COV_*prothom
• T_COV_*lbilirub
• T_COV_*y_age

Figure 15.10 shows the **Compute Time-Dependent Covariate** dialog box to declare the natural logarithm of T_ (an internal SPSS variable) to be the covariate of interest.

229

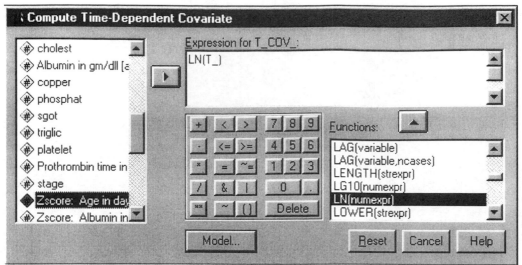

Figure 15.10 **Compute Time-Dependent Covariate** dialog box with expression shown.

Figure 15.11 shows the **Time- Dependent Cox Regression** dialog box filled in (reached by choosing **Model...** from the previous screen, Figure 15.10). Interactions with T_COV_ are formed by clicking on T_COV_ and one of the covariates (e.g., albumin) and then the **>a*b>** button.

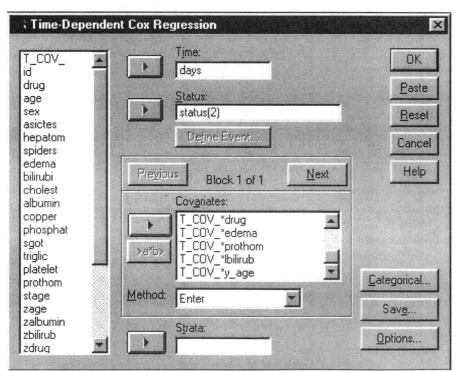

Figure 15.11   **Time-Dependent Cox Regression** dialog box.

Figure 15.12 shows the **Define Event** dialog box with STATUS=2 defined as an event (reached by choosing **Define Event...** from the screen shown in Figure 15.11).

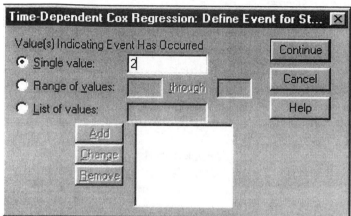

Figure 15.12   **Time-Dependent Cox Regression: Define Event** dialog box.

Clicking on **Continue** in the **Define Event** dialog box and then **OK** in the **Time-Dependent Cox Regression** dialog box produces Table 15.21 of *UMS*. Multicollinearity is evaluated through FACTOR, as per Section 6.1, listing the six covariates as variables.

15.2 COX REGRESSION SURVIVAL ANALYSIS

Figures 15.13 and 15.14 show the **Cox Regression** dialog boxes produced by choosing

>Analyze
  >Survival
    >Cox Regression...
      Time:
         • days
      Status:
         • status
         Define event...
            Value(s) Indicating Event Has Occurred:
               ⊙ Single value: 2
      Block 1 of 1
      Covariates:
         • albumin
         • edema
         • prothom
         • lbilirub
         • y_age
      Next
      Block 2 of 2
      Covariates:
         • drug

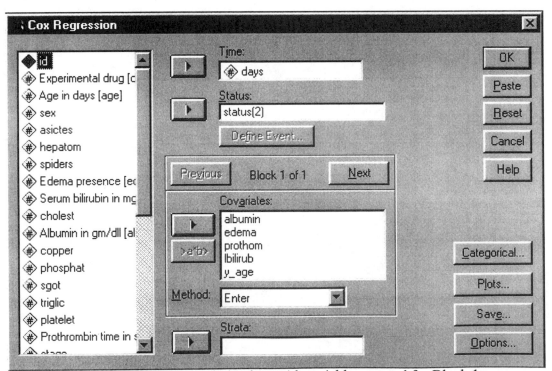

Figure 15.13   **Cox Regression** dialog box with variables entered for Block 1.

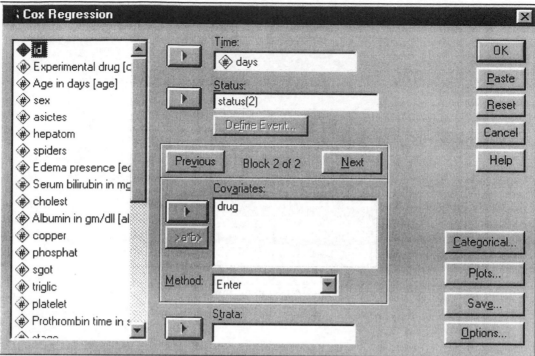

Figure 15.14   **Cox Regression** dialog box with variables entered for Block 2.

Clicking on **OK** produces Table 15.23 of *UMS* as output.

The plot of the survival function (Figure 15.2 in *UMS*) at mean of the five covariates is produced by running Cox regression from the setup in Figure 15.13 (covariates, excluding drug) after clicking on **Plots...** and selecting **Survival** from the **Plot type** list, as per Figure 15.15.

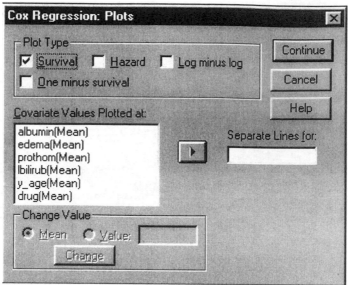

Figure 15.15   **Cox Regression: Plots** dialog box.

Chapter 16. Time Series Analysis

This chapter demonstrates time series analysis using SPSS for Windows for the complete example of Chapter 16 in *Using Multivariate Statistics*. The file to use is TIMESER.sav on the Internet site. (See Section 3.1 of Chapter 3 for detailed information on obtaining the SPSS files.) .

Number of incapacitating (A-level) injuries was tracked for 66 months before and 66 months after introduction of the Illinois seat belt law in 1985. Pre-intervention months are coded .00 for the variable labeled BELT, post-intervention months are labeled 1.00.

16.1   EVALUATION OF ASSUMPTIONS

Pre-analysis assumptions of homogeneity of variance and outliers are evaluated outside statistical programs as described in *UMS*. The logarithmic transformation of INJURY is accomplished as per Section 4.1.5, producing the variable LOG_INJ.

16.2   BASELINE MODEL IDENTIFICATION AND ESTIMATION

First, the series is restricted to pre-intervention baseline months by choosing,

>   >Data
>   >Select Cases
>   ⊙ If condition is satisfied
>   If...
>   • belt = 0
>   Unselected cases are
>   ⊙ Filtered

This produces Figures 16.1 and 16.2.

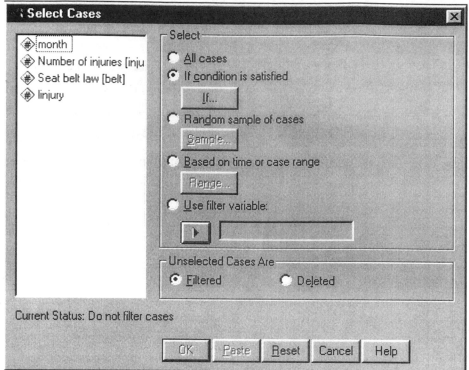

Figure 16.1   **Select Cases** dialog box.

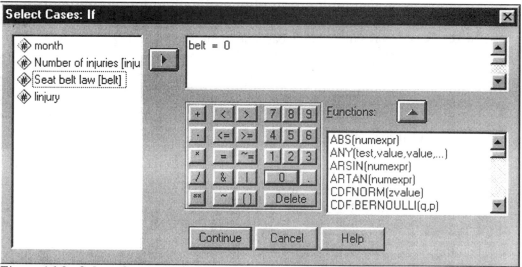

Figure 16.2 **Select Cases: If** dialog box.

ACF and PACF plots are produced using the following menu choices.

>Graphs
>Time Series
>Autocorrelations . . .
Variables:
• log_inj
Display
☑ Autocorrelations
☑ Partial autocorrelations
Options
Maximum number of lags: 25

This produces Figures 16.3 and 16.4.

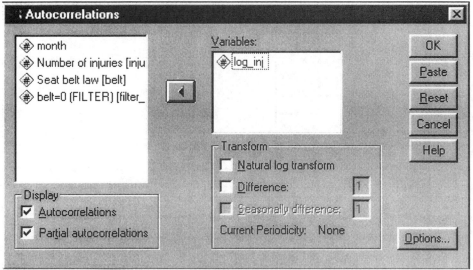

Figure 16.3   **Autocorrelations** dialog box.

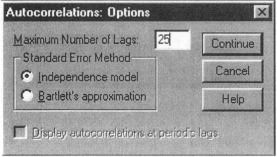

Figure 16.4   **Autocorrelations: Options**
dialog box.

Clicking on **Continue** and then **OK** produces *Output 16.1*.

Output 16.1   **ACF AND PACF PLOTS FOR THE TRANSFORMED PRE-SEAT BELT LAW TIME SERIES.**

```
MODEL:  MOD_1.


Autocorrelations:    LOG_INJ

       Auto- Stand.
Lag    Corr.  Err.   -1  -.75  -.5  -.25   0   .25   .5   .75   1     Box-Ljung   Prob.

  1    .618   .120                       .  ****.*******              26.354      .000
  2    .315   .119                       .  ****.*                    33.300      .000
  3   -.048   .118                        .  *    .                   33.466      .000
  4   -.257   .118                       *****    .                   38.232      .000
  5   -.335   .117                      **.****   .                   46.485      .000
  6   -.428   .116                    ****.****   .                   60.163      .000
  7   -.366   .115                      **.****   .                   70.353      .000
  8   -.354   .114                      **.****   .                   80.054      .000
  9   -.165   .113                        . ***   .                   82.209      .000
 10    .143   .112                           .  ***.                  83.856      .000
 11    .407   .111                           . ***.****               97.398      .000
 12    .666   .110                           . ***.*********          134.276     .000
 13    .426   .109                           . ***.*****              149.611     .000
 14    .208   .108                           . ****                   153.358     .000
 15   -.041   .107                         .  *   .                   153.510     .000
 16   -.204   .106                        ****   .                    157.245     .000
 17   -.244   .104                       *.***   .                    162.715     .000
 18   -.382   .103                     ****.***  .                    176.344     .000
 19   -.345   .102                      ***.***  .                    187.708     .000
 20   -.393   .101                     ****.***  .                    202.756     .000
 21   -.228   .100                       *.***|  .                    207.941     .000
 22    .014   .099                         . *|  .                    207.961     .000
 23    .270   .098                         . |***.*                   215.555     .000
 24    .497   .097                         . |***.******              241.903     .000
 25    .344   .096                         . |***.***                 254.868     .000


Plot Symbols:      Autocorrelations *       Two Standard Error Limits .

Total cases:  66    Computable first lags:  65
```
—

238

```
Partial Autocorrelations:   LOG_INJ

   Pr-Aut- Stand.
Lag  Corr.   Err. -1  -.75  -.5 -.25    0  .25   .5   .75   1
                    +----+----+----+----+----+----+----+----+

  1   .618   .123                  .    |****.*******
  2  -.108   .123                  .  **|    .
  3  -.322   .123                 *.****|    .
  4  -.112   .123                  .  **|    .
  5  -.044   .123                  .   *|    .
  6  -.282   .123                 *.****|    .
  7  -.060   .123                  .   *|    .
  8  -.209   .123                  .****|    .
  9   .034   .123                  .    |*   .
 10   .285   .123                  .    |****.*
 11   .174   .123                  .    |*** .
 12   .352   .123                  .    |****.**
 13  -.378   .123               ***.****|    .
 14  -.102   .123                  .  **|    .
 15   .106   .123                  .    |**  .
 16  -.058   .123                  .   *|    .
 17   .071   .123                  .    |*   .
 18  -.171   .123                  . ***|    .
 19  -.007   .123                  .    *    .
 20  -.084   .123                  .  **|    .
 21  -.035   .123                  .   *|    .
 22  -.059   .123                  .   *|    .
 23   .046   .123                  .    |*   .
 24   .057   .123                  .    |*   .
 25  -.077   .123                  .  **|    .

Plot Symbols:       Autocorrelations *     Two Standard Error Limits .

Total cases:  66     Computable first lags:  65
```

LOG_INJ

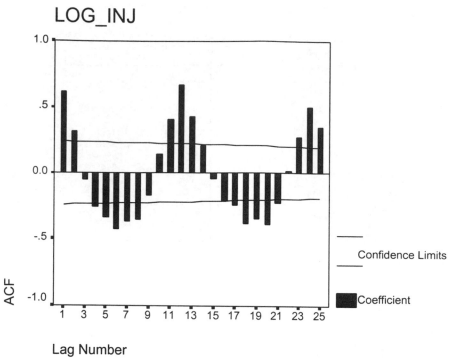

Lag Number

Confidence Limits

■ Coefficient

LOG_INJ

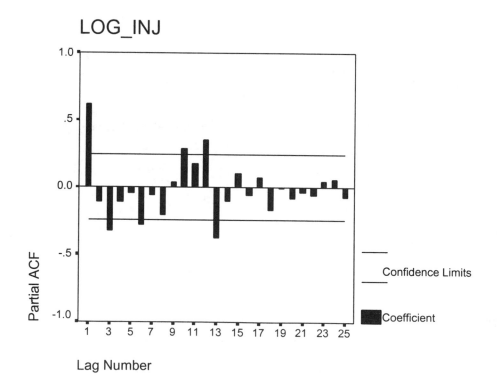

Lag Number

Confidence Limits

■ Coefficient

240

Before seasonal (lag 12) differencing can be accomplished, dates must be defined as follows:

> <u>D</u>ata
>> > D<u>e</u>fine Dates...
>>> <u>C</u>ases Are: Years, months
>>> <u>F</u>irst Case Is:
>>>> Year: 1980
>>>> Month: 1

This action produces Figure 16.5.

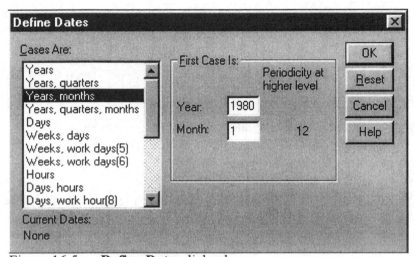

Figure 16.5   **Define Dates** dialog box.

Clicking on **OK** adds three variables to the data set: YEAR_, MONTH_, and DATE_. A portion of the data file is displayed in Figure 16.6. (Note that you may have to re-select baseline cases as per Figures 16.1 and 16.2.)

	month	injury	belt	log_inj	filter_$	year_	month_	date_
1	1.00	3637	.00	3.56	1	1980	1	JAN 1980
2	2.00	3241	.00	3.51	1	1980	2	FEB 1980
3	3.00	3244	.00	3.51	1	1980	3	MAR 1980
4	4.00	3666	.00	3.56	1	1980	4	APR 1980
5	5.00	4557	.00	3.66	1	1980	5	MAY 1980
6	6.00	4646	.00	3.67	1	1980	6	JUN 1980
7	7.00	4743	.00	3.68	1	1980	7	JUL 1980
8	8.00	4936	.00	3.69	1	1980	8	AUG 1980
9	9.00	4102	.00	3.61	1	1980	9	SEP 1980
10	10.00	4088	.00	3.61	1	1980	10	OCT 1980
11	11.00	3563	.00	3.55	1	1980	11	NOV 1980
12	12.00	4048	.00	3.61	1	1980	12	DEC 1980
13	13.00	3212	.00	3.51	1	1981	1	JAN 1981
14	14.00	3265	.00	3.51	1	1981	2	FEB 1981
15	15.00	3216	.00	3.51	1	1981	3	MAR 1981
16	16.00	3789	.00	3.58	1	1981	4	APR 1981
17	17.00	4306	.00	3.63	1	1981	5	MAY 1981
18	18.00	4357	.00	3.64	1	1981	6	JUN 1981
19	19.00	4332	.00	3.64	1	1981	7	JUL 1981
20	20.00	4570	.00	3.66	1	1981	8	AUG 1981
21	21.00	3884	.00	3.59	1	1981	9	SEP 1981
22	22.00	4111	.00	3.61	1	1981	10	OCT 1981
23	23.00	3755	.00	3.57	1	1981	11	NOV 1981

Figure 16.6   **SPSS Data editor** window showing creation of three new variables.

The following commands now produce ACF and PACF plots with differencing at lags 1 and 12.

>Graphs
>Time Series
>Autocorrelations . . .
Variables:
• log_inj
Display
☑ Autocorrelations
☑ Partial autocorrelations
Transform
☑ Difference: 1
☑ Seasonally difference: 1

Note that seasonal difference is set at 1, not 12. This produces Figure 16.7. The options remain
the same as before (maximum lags = 25).

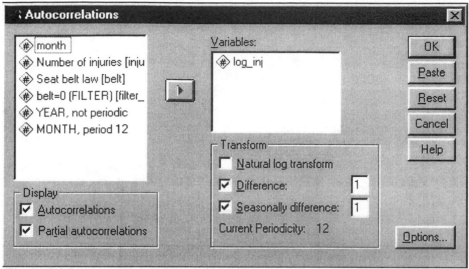

Figure 16.7   **Autocorrelations** dialog box.

Clicking on **OK** produces *Output 16.2.*

Output 16.2   ACF AND PACF PLOTS FOR THE PRE-SEAT BELT LAW TIME SERIES WITH LAG 1 AND 12 DIFFERENCING.

ACF

```
MODEL:  MOD_2.

13 case(s) will be lost due to differencing.
—


Autocorrelations:   LOG_INJ

Transformations:  difference (1), seasonal difference (1 at 12)

        Auto- Stand.
  Lag   Corr.  Err.  -1  -.75  -.5  -.25   0   .25  .5  .75   1   Box-Ljung  Prob.

    1  -.384  .134             ***.****  |      .           8.280    .004
    2  -.018  .132                 .   * .           8.298    .016
    3  -.050  .131                 .  * |  .           8.441    .038
    4   .177  .130                 .   |****.          10.306    .036
    5  -.359  .128            **.****  |      .          18.144    .003
    6   .172  .127                 .   |***  .          19.971    .003
    7   .024  .126                 .   *  .          20.009    .006
    8   .032  .124                 .   |*   .          20.074    .010
    9  -.011  .123                 .   *  .          20.082    .017
   10   .113  .121                 .   |**  .          20.949    .021
   11   .104  .120                 .   |**  .          21.699    .027
   12  -.413  .119             ***.****  |      .          33.829    .001
   13   .103  .117                 .   |**  .          34.609    .001
   14   .025  .116                 .   |*   .          34.657    .002
   15   .041  .114                 .   |*   .          34.789    .003
   16  -.137  .113                 . ***|  .          36.262    .003
   17   .268  .111                 .   |***.*          42.060    .001
   18  -.177  .110              ****|  .          44.678    .000
   19   .164  .108                 .   |***.          46.988    .000
   20  -.149  .106              .***|  .          48.940    .000
   21   .098  .105                 .   |**  .          49.817    .000
   22  -.222  .103              ****|  .          54.447    .000
   23   .141  .101                 .   |***.          56.383    .000
   24  -.081  .100               .  **|  .          57.040    .000
   25   .192  .098                 .   |****          60.885    .000

Plot Symbols:      Autocorrelations *     Two Standard Error Limits .

Total cases:  66     Computable first lags after differencing:  52
—


Partial Autocorrelations:   LOG_INJ

Transformations:  difference (1), seasonal difference (1 at 12)
```

244

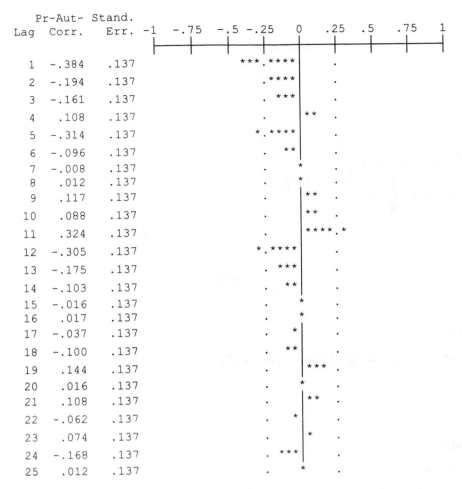

```
      Pr-Aut- Stand.
Lag   Corr.   Err.  -1  -.75  -.5  -.25   0   .25   .5   .75    1
                     ├────┼─────┼─────┼─────┼─────┼─────┼─────┼───┤
  1   -.384   .137                   ***.****│       .
  2   -.194   .137                      .****│       .
  3   -.161   .137                      . ***│       .
  4    .108   .137                      .    │**     .
  5   -.314   .137                     *.****│       .
  6   -.096   .137                      .  **│       .
  7   -.008   .137                      .    *       .
  8    .012   .137                      .    *       .
  9    .117   .137                      .    │**     .
 10    .088   .137                      .    │**     .
 11    .324   .137                      .    │****.* 
 12   -.305   .137                     *.****│       .
 13   -.175   .137                      . ***│       .
 14   -.103   .137                      .  **│       .
 15   -.016   .137                      .    *       .
 16    .017   .137                      .    *       .
 17   -.037   .137                      .   *│       .
 18   -.100   .137                      .  **│       .
 19    .144   .137                      .    │***    .
 20    .016   .137                      .    *       .
 21    .108   .137                      .    │**     .
 22   -.062   .137                      .   *│       .
 23    .074   .137                      .    │*      .
 24   -.168   .137                      . ***│       .
 25    .012   .137                      .    *       .
```

Plot Symbols: Autocorrelations *   Two Standard Error Limits .

Total cases: 66   Computable first lags after differencing: 52

245

LOG_INJ

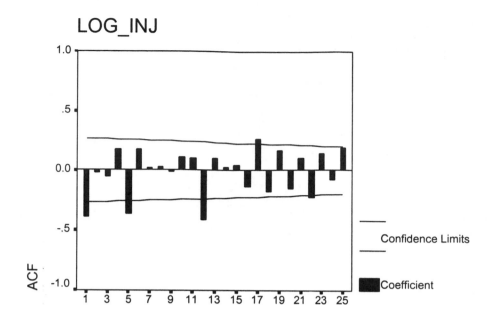

Lag Number

Transforms: difference (1), seasonal difference (1, period 12)

LOG_INJ

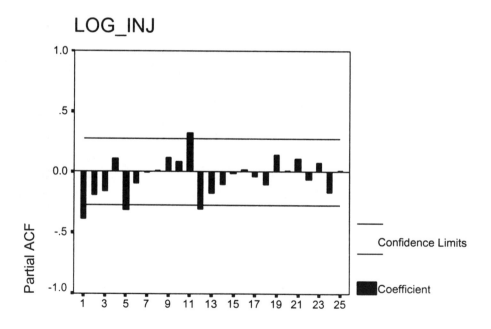

Lag Number

Transforms: difference (1), seasonal difference (1, period 12)

246

The ARIMA $(1, 1, 1)(1, 1, 1)_{12}$ model is produced by the following choices.

>Analyze
>Time Series
>ARIMA . . .
Dependent:
• log_inj
Model
Autoregressive   p: 1   sp: 1
Difference   d: 1   sd: 1
Moving Average   q: 1   sq: 1

This produces Figure 16.8. Note that the constant is not included in the model; recall that differencing precludes inclusion of the constant. Note also that a differenced variable is not created outside the model here; differencing is done within the ARIMA menu for seasonal models.

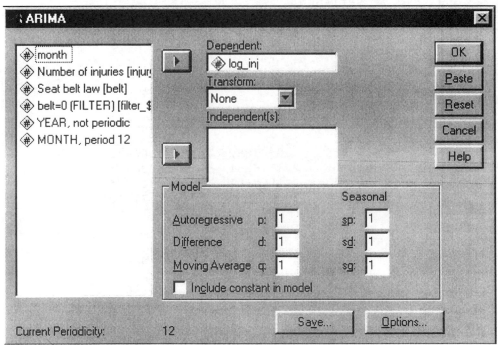

Figure 16.8   **ARIMA** dialog box of time series analysis.

Clicking on **OK** produces *Output 16.3.*

247

```
MODEL:  MOD_8
_
```

Model Description:

```
Variable:  LOG_INJ
Regressors: NONE
```

```
Non-seasonal differencing: 1
    Seasonal differencing: 1
Length of Seasonal Cycle: 12
```

FINAL PARAMETERS:

```
Number of residuals  53
Standard error        .02591506
Log likelihood       115.33781
AIC                 -222.67561
SBC                 -214.79445
```

Analysis of Variance:

	DF	Adj. Sum of Squares	Residual Variance
Residuals	49	.03970952	.00067159

Variables in the Model:

	B	SEB	T-RATIO	APPROX. PROB.
AR1	.08972055	.23686161	.3787889	.70648100
MA1	.63331377	.20313896	3.1176381	.00304866
SAR1	.02373779	.27647043	.0858601	.93192747
SMA1	.76808356	.48243847	1.5920861	.11779680

Covariance Matrix:

	AR1	MA1	SAR1	SMA1
AR1	.05610342	.04000577	.00932506	.00587869
MA1	.04000577	.04126544	.00749199	.00336522
SAR1	.00932506	.00749199	.07643590	.10769460
SMA1	.00587869	.00336522	.10769460	.23274688

Correlation Matrix:

	AR1	MA1	SAR1	SMA1
AR1	1.0000000	.8314474	.1423995	.0514451
MA1	.8314474	1.0000000	.1333998	.0343382
SAR1	.1423995	.1333998	1.0000000	.8074271

```
SMA1       .0514451    .0343382    .8074271   1.0000000
```

The following new variables are being created:

```
   Name           Label

   FIT_5          Fit for LOG_INJ from ARIMA, MOD_8 NOCON
   ERR_5          Error for LOG_INJ from ARIMA, MOD_8 NOCON
   LCL_5          95% LCL for LOG_INJ from ARIMA, MOD_8 NOCON
   UCL_5          95% UCL for LOG_INJ from ARIMA, MOD_8 NOCON
   SEP_5          SE of fit for LOG_INJ from ARIMA, MOD_8 NOCON
```

Output is not entirely consistent with that of Table 16.24 in *UMS*. The most serious discrepancy is the failure of the SMA1 parameter (seasonal MA, lag 12, corresponding to MA2,1 of Table 16.24) to reach statistical significance: APPROX. PROB. = .118... . Although the Parameter Estimate is higher, so is the standard error (SEB). Nevertheless, the $(1, 1, 1)(1, 1, 1)_{12}$ model is retained to maintain consistency with *UMS*. This model actually produced significant seasonal as well as local MA components in the SPSS baseline run.

16.3   BASELINE MODEL DIAGNOSIS

A run of the $(1, 1, 1)(1, 1, 1)_{12}$ model of *Output 16.3* saves residuals in the data set; the variable labeled ERR_1 contains the residuals. The normal probability residuals plot is produced by choosing:

>Graphs
>>P-P...
>>>Variables:
>>>>• ERR_1

Remaining menu choices are left in default modes, as seen in Figure 16.9.

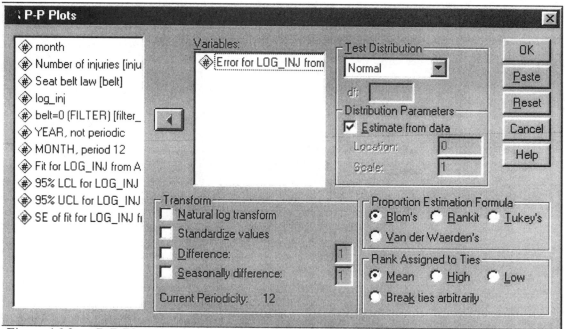

Figure 16.9   **P-P Plots** (probability plots) dialog box.

This produces Figures 16.10 and 16.11.

Normal P-P Plot of Error for LOG_INJ f

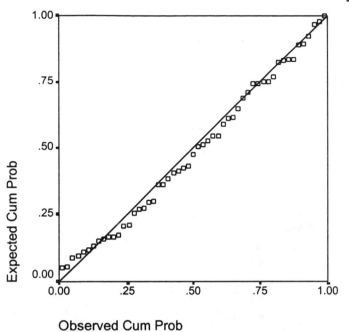

Figure 16.10   **Normal probability plot of Error for Log_INJf.**

Detrended Normal P-P Plot of Error for LOG_

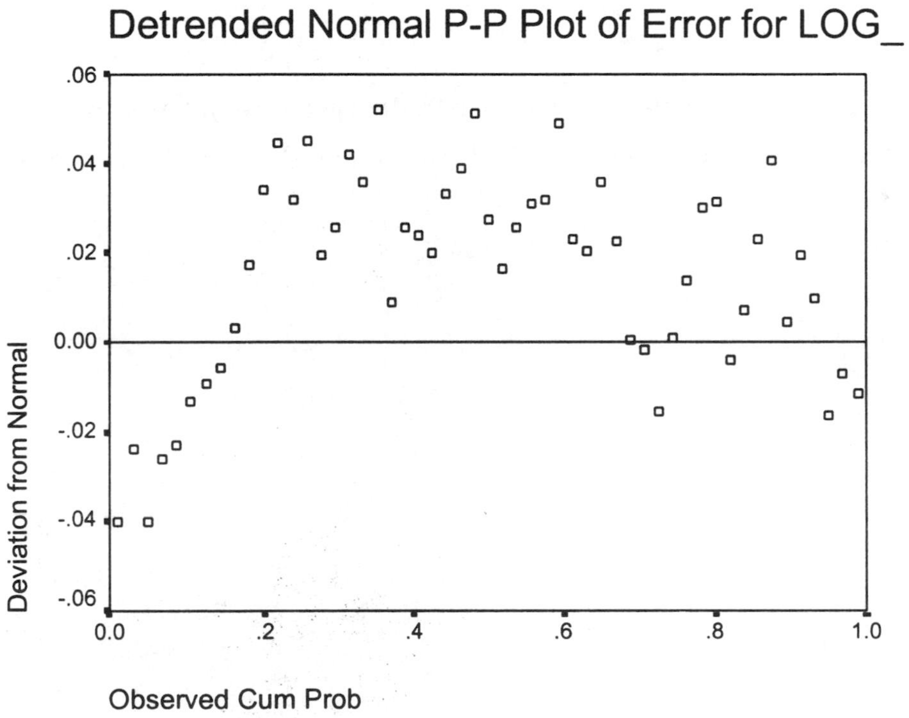

Figure 16.11   **Detrended probability plot of Error for Log_INJf.**

The normal probability plot of residuals is quite consistent with that of Figure 16.13 in *UMS*. As for that analysis, residuals for the $(0, 1, 1)(0, 1, 1)_{12}$ were not noticeably different.

16.4   INTERVENTION ANALYSIS

After changing selection so that all 132 cases are used, you are ready to create the $(0, 1, 1)(0, 1, 1)_{12}$ model by choosing the following:

```
>Analyze
    >Time Series
        >ARIMA . . .
            Dependent:
                • log_inj
            Independent:
                • belt
                • month
            Model
                Autoregressive    p:  0      sp:  0
                Difference        d:  1      sd:  1
                Moving Average    q:  1      sq:  1
```

Thus, for this model, the intervention is specified in the **Independent(s):** box as BELT, and MONTH is added as another IV, as shown in Figure 16.12. Clicking on **OK** produces *Output 16.4.*

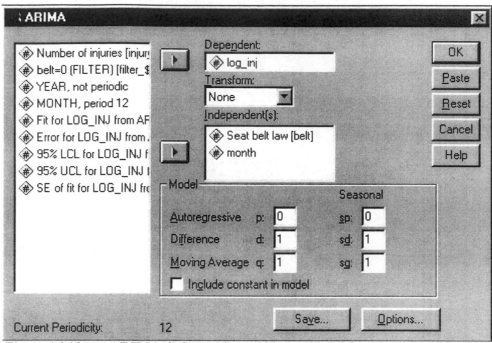

Figure 16.12   **ARIMA** dialog with variables and model settings shown.

Output 16.4   **STEP INTERVENTION TEST OF ARIMA (0, 1, 1)(0, 1, 1)$_{12}$ MODEL OF INJURY DATA.**


```
MODEL:  MOD_14

Model Description:

Variable:   LOG_INJ
Regressors: BELT
            MONTH

Non-seasonal differencing: 1
    Seasonal differencing: 1
Length of Seasonal Cycle: 12



FINAL PARAMETERS:

Number of residuals  119
Standard error       .02462008
Log likelihood       264.48019
AIC                  -520.96038
SBC                  -509.84389
```

Analysis of Variance:

	DF	Adj. Sum of Squares	Residual Variance
Residuals	115	.08118155	.00060615

Variables in the Model:

	B	SEB	T-RATIO	APPROX. PROB.
MA1	.60637151	.07438476	8.1518246	.00000000
SMA1	.88749783	.14765177	6.0107497	.00000002
BELT	-.06255826	.01948620	-3.2103874	.00171867
MONTH	.00262171	.00218700	1.1987654	.23308358

Covariance Matrix:

	MA1	SMA1
MA1	.00553309	-.00111696
SMA1	-.00111696	.02180105

Correlation Matrix:

	MA1	SMA1
MA1	1.0000000	-.1016984
SMA1	-.1016984	1.0000000

Regressor Covariance Matrix:

	BELT	MONTH
BELT	.00037971	.00000051
MONTH	.00000051	.00000478

—

Regressor Correlation Matrix:

	BELT	MONTH
BELT	1.0000000	.0120064
MONTH	.0120064	1.0000000

The following new variables are being created:

Name	Label
FIT_2	Fit for LOG_INJ from ARIMA, MOD_14 NOCON
ERR_2	Error for LOG_INJ from ARIMA, MOD_14 NOCON
LCL_2	95% LCL for LOG_INJ from ARIMA, MOD_14 NOCON
UCL_2	95% UCL for LOG_INJ from ARIMA, MOD_14 NOCON
SEP_2	SE of fit for LOG_INJ from ARIMA, MOD_14 NOCON

Parameter estimates diverge from those in Table 16.25 in *UMS*, but are not substantively different. Here, the antilog of the intervention parameter is $10^{-0.06255826} = 0.87$, indicating a reduction of about 13% in A-level injuries.

Residuals for this model may be checked as per Figures 16.9 through 16.11. Medians before and after intervention may be calculated by choosing the following SPSS commands, and as shown in Figure 16.13.

>Analyze
      >Reports
          >Case Summaries . . .
            Variables:
                • injury
            Grouping Variable(s):
                • belt
          ☑ Display cases   [optional]
              Statistics...
                  Cell Statistics
                      Number of Cases
                      Median

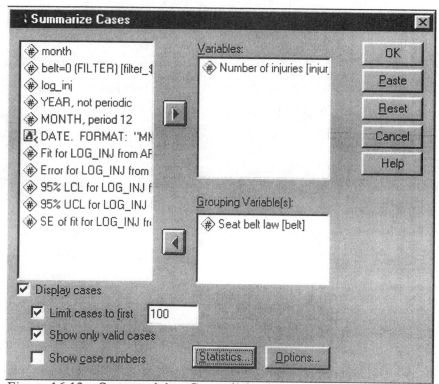

Figure 16.13 **Summarizing Cases** dialog box.

Deselecting the **Display cases** box reduces the output. Clicking on **Continue** and then **OK** produces *Output 16.5*.

Output 16.5   **DESCRIPTIVE STATISTICS FOR UNTRANSFORMED TIME SERIES DATA.**

Summarize

Case Processing Summary

	Cases					
	Included		Excluded		Total	
	N	Percent	N	Percent	N	Percent
Number of injuries * Seat belt law	132	100.0%	0	.0%	132	100.0%

Case Summaries

Number of injuries

Seat belt law	N	Median
No	66	3801.50
Yes	66	2791.50
Total	132	3146.00

Effect size for the ARIMA intervention model is estimated using Equation 16.14 of *UMS*, again using a model without intervention parameter estimates in the denominator. The entire series run without intervention parameters (not shown) produces Residual Variance = 0.0006, so that $SS_y = (.0006)(114) = 0.0684$. The Residual Variance from *Output 16.4* is .00067, so that $SS_y = (.00067)(112) = 0.0750$. Thus,

$$R^2 = 1 - \frac{0.0684}{0.0750} = .09$$

Note that this value is somewhat higher than that produced in Section 16.7.4.2 in *UMS*.